CELESTIAL NAVIGATION WORK FORMS

For All Sights and Tables, with Complete Instructions and Examples

by

David Burch

STARPATH

Contents

Copyright © 2018 by David F. Burch

All rights reserved.

ISBN 978-0-914025-62-7

Published by

Starpath Publications

3050 NW 63rd Street, Seattle, WA 98107

Manufactured in the United States of America

www.starpathpublications.com

Overview of Starpath Work Forms

Not all celestial navigators use work forms to help with the paperwork, but I think it's fair to say that most do. Or they at least like to have the forms at hand just in case they are needed (even very experienced navigators). There are a lot of steps in some of the reductions, and we may have to do the work when we are very tired and not feeling well, as the boat rocks around in the seas. Having a guide that takes us step by step, with little thought required, can be a blessing. So even if you do not use them routinely, it is good practice to add them to your checklist and have at least one of each type tucked away in the *Almanac*. Also, these days we rely mainly on GPS; so we might be rusty when we need to do the sights. These forms will remind you of the steps involved and guide you though any sight reduction. Those who want to use them routinely can duplicate the ones needed most from this book.

There are one or more forms for all routine sights using various sight reduction methods. Each has annotated step-by-step instructions for filling out the forms, which in themselves are a good refresher for the process. After a little practice, the forms are all we need to work through the sight reductions.

The main Form 104 for all sights has three levels of guidance. The long instructions with details of each step, the short instructions, which abbreviates the steps, and finally the forms themselves, which are organized in a logical, numbered format that guides you though the process.

After teaching celestial navigation for 40 years using our basic Form 104, we have heard back many times from navigators who have been away from the subject for a long time, who told us how easy it was to recall the paperwork with the use of these forms. This was, of course, an intention of the forms, along with the main design criteria that they allow all sights to be done essentially the same way. Another goal was to have a place to write in every step of the process, and to have some reasonable element of smooth flow throughout. Alternative designs that one sees are typically vertical strip forms that usually do not meet any of these criteria. Form 104 and the detailed instructions included here are effectively a short course in celestial navigation.

Our Form 106 for the Nautical Almanac Office (NAO) Tables included in every *Nautical Almanac* are especially valuable, because the instructions for the process given in the *Nautical Almanac* are difficult to follow. As a result of that problem, these valuable sight reduction tables have not been used as much as they deserve. Some instructors go so far as to ridicule the NAO Tables for their complexity, driving new users away before they even get to try them. Misguided magazine articles have not helped. Our Form 106 makes the process very simple, and with just a few samples worked, you will be doing them routinely with nothing but the form to look at.

The NAO Tables have a great virtue these days when cel nav is often just a back up to GPS. Since there is a full set of the NAO Tables in every *Nautical Almanac*, you just need to buy one book to have a complete solution. Pub 249, and especially Pub 229, are large, heavy books when it comes to stowage on a small boat at sea. Also if you choose to do sight reduction by computation, then the NAO Tables as part of the Almanac are a natural back up.

Likewise with the more basic reductions of Latitude at LAN and Latitude by *Polaris*, we have longer forms (Form 107 and 110) with more details of the process along with a combined short form (117) to use once the procedures are recalled.

About This Booklet

This booklet explains the motivation of the individual forms and provides detailed instructions on using them with numerical examples. We also include notes on the history of the NAO Tables and discussion of the relative merits of the various sight reduction methods. There is also a set of blank forms provided of each type, the most of which being our primary Forms 104 and 106.

The main goal of this booklet is to provide the instructions and examples with enough printed forms to allow them to be evaluated by those who do not have ready access to a printer. Blank forms in PDF format suitable for printing are available at no charge.

Where to Download Free Forms

These forms are used in our textbook *Celestial Navigation: A Complete Home Study Course,* as well as in our Online Course in Celestial Navigation. To support these training programs and the marine navigation community more generally, we offer a free, complete set of the forms in a PDF file that can be printed for further use. These and other resources are available on the support page for our text at:

www.starpath.com/celnavbook.

Readers are welcome to download and reproduce these forms for their personal use.

Note to Ebook Readers

The ebook editions of this booklet are intended only to provide a convenient reference to the discussions, instructions, and numerical examples used in the forms. The forms themselves are available from the link above. This way the instructions can be kept in a phone or tablet for quick reference as needed, and only the chosen forms need to be reproduced. Also, the design of the forms alone may be all that is needed to solve the reductions using a blank piece of paper.

FORM 104
All bodies, using Pub 249 or Pub 229

Sun Sights with Form 104

BOX 1–Sight Data

Record the watch time (WT), watch date, log reading, celestial body, measured index correction, and sextant reading (Hs) for the sight. Find the watch error (WE) and the zone description (ZD) of the watch from WWV radio broadcasts or chronometer logbook, and apply these to WT to get the universal time (UTC) of the sight. Use the extra space provided to adjust time and date if necessary. Choose and record a LOP line of position (LOP) label for the sight. From your dead reckoning (DR) track on a chart or plotting sheet, figure your DR position (DR-Lat and DR-Lon) and log reading at the time of the sight. Record your height of eye (HE) for the sight.

BOX 2–*Nautical Almanac* Daily Pages

From the *Nautical Almanac* daily pages, record the Greenwich hour angle (GHA-hr) and declination (Dec-hr) of the sun at the exact hour of the UTC. Record the declination d-value, and label it "+" if declination is increasing with time, or "-" if decreasing. Cross out the spaces for v-value and HP; they do not apply to the sun.

BOX 3–Increments and Corrections

From the increments and corrections pages of the *Nautical Almanac*, record the sun's increment of GHA (GHA-m,s) for the minutes and seconds part of the UTC. Also record the d-correction to the declination based on the d-value given in Box 2. Cross out the SHA or v-correction space; these do not apply to the sun.

Add GHA-hr to GHA-m,s to find GHA and record it. Apply the d-corr to Dec-hr to find Dec and record it. The sign (±) of d-corr is the same as that of d-value. Use the extra space provided to adjust minutes to less than 60 if necessary. You now have the GHA and Dec that apply for your precise UTC. For later use, record the degrees part of the declination (Dec-deg) in Box 4 with a prominent N or S label, and also record the minutes part (Dec-min) in Box 5.

Assumed Position and Hour Angle

Figure the assumed longitude (a-Lon) from your DR-Lon and the minutes part of GHA. In western longitudes, it should be the one longitude that lies within 30' of your DR-Lon that has the same minutes as the minutes part of GHA. In eastern longitudes, it should be the one longitude that lies within 30' of your DR-Lon that has minutes equal to 60 minus the minutes part of GHA. Record a-Lon below GHA and also in Box 6. Figure the local hour angle (LHA) from:

$$LHA = GHA - a\text{-}Lon(W)$$

in western longitudes or

$$LHA = GHA + a\text{-}Lon(E)$$

in eastern longitudes. With the proper choice of a-Lon, LHA will always be in whole degrees with no minutes left over. Record LHA in Box 4.

Choose the assumed latitude (a-Lat) as your DR-Lat rounded off to the nearest whole degree. Record a-Lat in Box 4 with a prominent N or S label. Also record a-Lat in Box 6.

BOX 4 and BOX 5–Sight Reduction Tables

Box 4 now contains all data needed to enter the Sight Reduction Tables, Pubs. 249 or 229. Same or Contrary Name labels of Dec and a-Lat are clear at a glance.

From the Sight Reduction Tables, record in Box 5 the tabulated value of the calculated altitude (tab Hc), the d-value with its tabulated sign (±), and the azimuth angle (Z).

Convert the azimuth angle (Z) to the azimuth (Zn) using the rules on the work form (also given on each page of the Sight Reduction Tables) and record it in Box 6. CAUTION: For "high-altitude" sights, meaning Hc above 70° or so, you should interpolate for Z to account for the minutes part of Dec. Use:

$$Z = Z(\text{Dec-deg}) + dZ,$$

where

$$dZ = [Z(\text{Dec-deg} + 1°) - Z(\text{Dec-deg})] \times (\text{Dec-min})/60.$$

Hs to Ho

The upper right side of the work form is used for converting the sextant altitude (Hs) to the observed altitude (Ho). Altitude corrections are inside the covers of the *Nautical Almanac*. Record the dip correction and apply dip and index corr to Hs to get the apparent altitude (Ha).

Cross out the additional altitude corr space and the upper limb moon space; these do not apply to the sun.

Record the altitude correction for the sun and apply it to Ha to get Ho. Compare Hc and Ho in the space provided above Box 6. Subtract the smaller from the larger to get the altitude intercept (a). Extra space is provided to rewrite Ho or Hc if necessary for this subtraction. Choose the label, A for Away or T for Toward, which is beside the larger of Hc or Ho, and record the a-value and mark its label in Box 6.

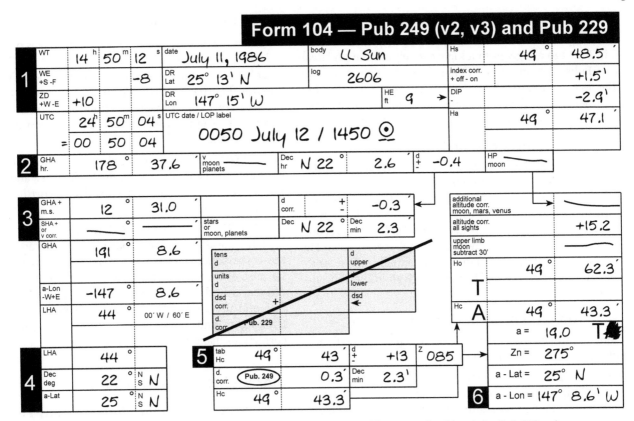

Figure 104-1. *Sight reduction of the sun using Form 104 and Pub 249. The crossed out box is for Pub 229 only.*

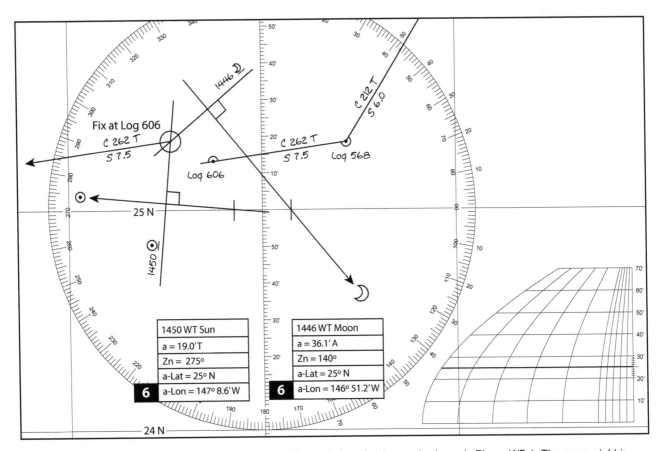

Figure 104-2. *Plot of a celestial fix from a sun and moon sight. The work form for the sun is shown in Figure WF-1. The moon sight is shown worked out on the next page in Figure 104-3.*

Pub 249 Versus Pub 229

Although the tables are arranged differently and the values in Pub 229 are given to a higher precision, the practical use of Pubs. 249 and 229 differs only in the determination of the d-correction to tab Hc. In Pub 249 this is done in one step, whereas in Pub 229 this must be done in several steps. The extra steps are required for the extra precision.

d-Corr from Pub 249

From Table 5 of Pub 249, record the d-correction. It depends on the d-value and Dec-min (recorded together in Box 5 for convenience). Apply this d-corr to tab Hc to find Hc and record it. The sign (±) of d-corr is the same as the sign of the d-value given in the Sight Reduction Tables. Also record Hc above Box 6. You can interpolate the d-correction to Hc for the minutes of the declination to potentially gain a tenth or two in precision. (Use of Pub 229 is given in the star and planet examples.)

BOX 6–Plotting the Line of Position

Box 6 now contains all data needed to plot the LOP on a plotting sheet. Plotting procedure:

(1) Set up a plotting sheet with mid-latitude equal to a-Lat and mid-longitude equal to a-Lon rounded off to the nearest whole degree. Plot a point at the assumed position (a-Lat, a-Lon).

(2) Draw a line through this point in the direction of Zn (this is the true bearing of the object at the sight time). We call this line the "azimuth line."

(3) Put a mark on the azimuth line at a distance of "a" nautical miles from the assumed position, where "a" is the a-value in Box 6 expressed in minutes of arc (get this distance from the latitude scale on the plotting sheet). Mark the point on the azimuth line in the direction toward Zn, when "a" is labeled T; go the opposite direction along the azimuth line (away from Zn) when "a" is labeled A.

(4) Finally, draw a line perpendicular to the azimuth line passing through the point just marked. This perpendicular line is your LOP. This sight and sight reduction have told you that you are located somewhere on this line. Label the LOP with the name of the celestial body, the log reading, and the UTC.

Moon Sights with Form 104

BOX 2–*Nautical Almanac* Daily Pages

From the *Nautical Almanac* daily pages, record the Greenwich Hour Angle (GHA-hr), v-value, declination (Dec-hr), d-value, and horizontal parallax (HP) for the moon at the exact hour of the UTC. These values are simply transferred to the work form in the exact order they are listed in the *Nautical Almanac*. Figure and record the label of the d-value: label it "+" if declination is increasing with time, or "-" if it is decreasing. CAUTION: The d-value label is found from the trend in *declination* not from the trend in the d-value itself.

BOX 3–Increments and Corrections

From the increments and corrections pages of the *Nautical Almanac*, record the moon's increment of GHA (GHA-m,s) for the minutes and seconds part of the UTC. Also record the d-correction to the declination (based on the d-value given in Box 2) and the v-correction (based on the v-value of Box 2). Cross out the space label "SHA+"; for the moon this space contains v-corr.

Add GHA-hr, GHA-m,s, and v-corr to find GHA and record it. Add the d-corr to Dec-hr to find Dec and record it. For the moon v-corr is always positive; d-corr has the same sign as d-value.

ALL THE REST IS THE SAME AS FOR SUN LINES except that the altitude corrections for the moon are taken from the corresponding moon tables in the *Nautical Almanac*. Because of the way the tables are organized, the moon's additional altitude correction (needed for all moon sights) must be found after finding the altitude correction. For upper limb noon sights (and only for these) subtract 30' from the altitude corrections using the labeled space provided.

Star Sights with Form 104

BOX 2–*Nautical Almanac* Daily Pages

From the *Nautical Almanac* daily pages, record in Box 2 the Greenwich Hour Angle (GHA-hr) of Aries at the exact hour of the UTC. Record the declination (Dec) and sidereal hour angle (SHA) of the star in Box 3. Cross out the spaces for v-value, Dec-hr, d-value, and HP; they do not apply to stars.

BOX 3–Increments and Corrections

From the increments and corrections pages of the *Nautical Almanac*, record the Aries increment of GHA (GHA-m,s) for the minutes and seconds part of the UTC. Cross out the d-corr space; stars have no d-corr. And cross out the space label "v-corr"; for stars this space contains SHA.

Add GHA-hr, GHA-m,s, and SHA to find the GHA of the star and record it. Use the extra space provided to adjust minutes to less than 60 and degrees to less than 360, if necessary.

ALL THE REST IS THE SAME AS FOR SUN LINES except that the altitude correction for stars is taken from the stars and planets table instead of the sun table.

d-Corr from Pub 229

Pub 229 can be used to reduce any sight (Pub 249 is only for declinations less than 29°). It provides a higher precision (0.1' on Hc) compared to Pub 249 (1'), but it takes a few extra steps to obtain this. In Form 104, we use the middle box for these extra steps to finding the d-correction to Hc. The star and planet sights shown in Figures 5 and 6 use this method.

First, record the tens and units parts of the d-value in the spaces above Box 5. From the Interpolation Table on the inside covers of Pub 229, record the tens and units corrections with their tabulated signs (±) in the spaces next to the d-value parts. These corrections depend on the d-value parts and on Dec-min, which is called the *declination increment* in Pub 229. Add the tens and units corrections to get the d-corr and then apply this correction to tab Hc to get the final Hc. Also record Hc in the space above Box 6.

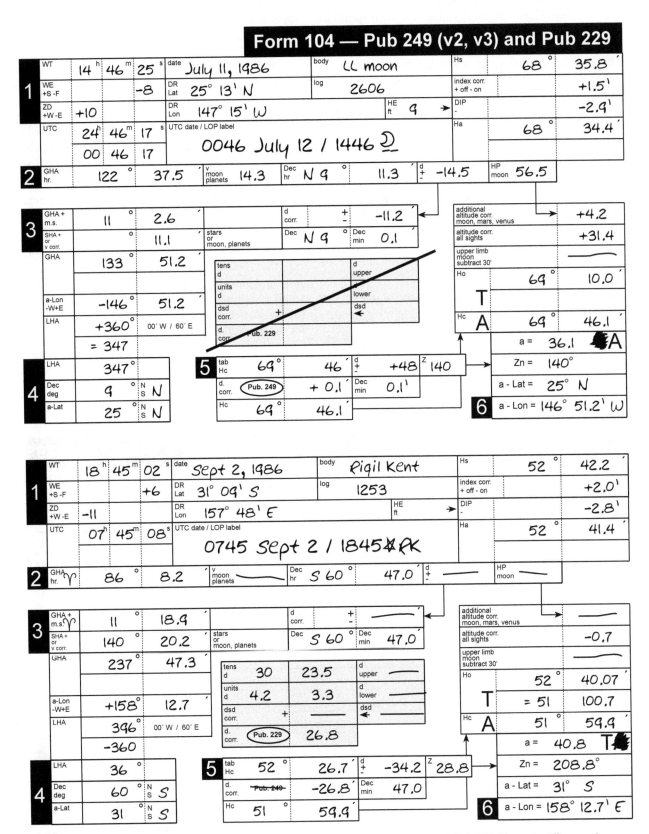

Figure 104-4. *Moon (top) and star (bottom, Rigil Kentarus) sight reductions using Form 104 and Pub 229. The only difference between Pub 229 and Pub 249 for this form is the box in the middle of the form used to figure the d correction to Hc.*

If (when first recording tab Hc, d, and Z) the d-value is listed with an asterisk (*), a further correction is needed for maximum precision. Proceed as above, but also record the d-values just above and just below (d-upper and d-lower) the tabulated d-value. These are the d-values that correspond to Dec values 1° above and below the Dec-deg recorded in Box 4. Next figure the *double second difference* (dsd), which equals the difference between d-upper and d-lower, and record it. Find the dsd-correction in the small table, inset next to the tens and units corrections table. Record this small dsd correction and add it to the tens and units correction to find the final d-corr. The dsd-corr is always positive, regardless of the sign of the tens and units corrections.

NOTE: dsd corrections are only needed for high-altitude sights, and for these you must interpolate for the azimuth angle Z as explained in the earlier caution note. Hence an asterisk signaling a dsd correction is also your signal to interpolate for Z. Pub 249 does not have this built-in warning.

Planet Sights with Form 104

BOX 2–*Nautical Almanac* Daily Pages

From the *Nautical Almanac* daily pages, record the Greenwich Hour Angle (GHA-hr) and declination (Dec-hr) of the planet at the exact hour of the UTC. Record the declination d-value, and label it "+" if declination is increasing with

time, or "-" if decreasing. Record the v-value, it is positive for all planets except Venus, which can sometimes be negative. If it is negative, it is listed as such, and the v-corr found from it should be subtracted. Cross out the space for HP; it does not apply to planets.

BOX 3–Increments and Corrections

From the increments and corrections pages of the *Nautical Almanac*, record the planet's increment of GHA (GHA-m,s) for the minutes and seconds part of the UTC. Also, record the d-correction to the declination (based on the d-value of Box 2) and the v-correction to the GHA (based on the v-value in Box 2). Cross out the space label "SHA"; for planets this space contains v-corr. Add GHA-hr, GHA-m,s, and v-corr to find GHA and record it.

If v-value is negative for Venus, the v-corr is negative. Apply d-corr to Dec-hr to find Dec and record it. The sign of d-corr is the same as that of d-value.

ALL THE REST IS THE SAME AS FOR SUN LINES except that the altitude correction for planets is taken from the stars and planets table instead of the sun table. Also there is a small additional altitude correction in the *Nautical Almanac* for the planets Mars and Venus. A labeled space is provided for this additional correction.

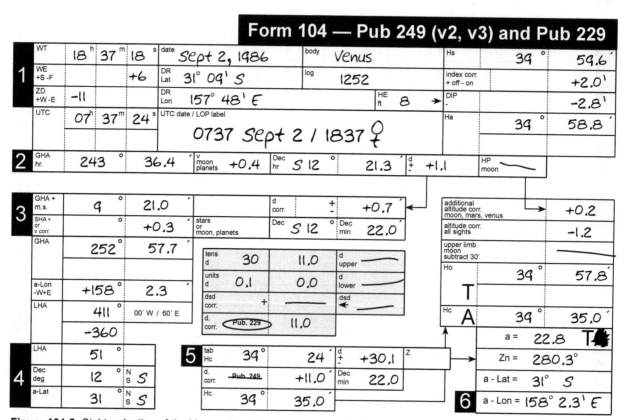

Figure 104-5. *Sight reduction of the Venus using Form 104 and Pub 229. The only difference between Pub 229 and Pub 249 for this form is the box in the middle of the form used to figure the d correction to Hc.*

FORM 106
All bodies, using NAO Tables

About the NAO Tables

Starting in 1989, there was a significant change in the available tables for celestial navigation. Prior to then, Sight Reduction Tables were usually chosen from Pub 249 (most popular with yachtsmen) and Pub 229, which is required on USCG license exams. The latter have more precision, but this extra precision would rarely affect the final accuracy of a celestial fix from a moving vessel in routine circumstances. Pub 229 is much heavier, more expensive, and requires a couple extra steps.

In 1989 the Nautical Almanac Office (NAO) began to include a set of Sight Reduction Tables at the back of the *Nautical Almanac*. Now when you buy an almanac, you get a set of Sight Reduction Tables with it, even if you don't intend to use these tables. As always, the almanac data must be replaced each new year with a new almanac, but the Sight Reduction Tables they include each year will be the same. Like all standard Sight Reduction Tables, these are not dated and can be used for sights from any year. We coined the nickname "NAO Tables" at the time, and it seems to have stuck.

The tables are very short, but they will reduce any sight, and provide the same Hc precision as the Pub 249 tables (0.5', rounded to nearest 1') and the same azimuth precision (0.05°, rounded to nearest 0.1°) as the Pub 229 tables. The price we pay, however, for a free set of concise tables is the amount of work necessary to get the numbers out of them.

All Sight Reduction Tables start with Lat, LHA, and Dec and end up with Hc and Zn. With Pub 249, the answer is obtained in two steps. With Pub 229, it takes three steps, sometimes four, and with the new NAO tables it always takes four steps with some adding and subtracting between the steps.

At first glance, the NAO Tables are awkward to use and not an attractive alternative to Pub 249. There are several reasons, however, to not rule them out too quickly. First, they will always be there. As of 1989, everyone has them, like it or not. Second, celestial itself is a backup navigation method to most sailors these days. Most rely on GPS, only using celestial to test it or to replace it if it fails. Sailors who rely on celestial daily, on the other hand, usually do not use tables at all, but instead do all the paperwork with a calculator. In short,

traditional navigation using tables is becoming less and less common. Since we are not using tables often, it is not so bad that the tables take a bit longer to use.

In short, if we take the time to learn these new tables and are comfortable with the knowledge that we can use them if we need to, we can save space, money, and complexity in the long run by not having to bother with various sources of tables. With this in mind, we have developed a work form that makes the use of these tables considerably easier than just following the instructions given in the almanac. With the use of our work form, the NAO tables do not take much longer than Pub 249 does for this step of the work. Naturally, the first few times go slowly, but after a few examples it becomes automatic and easy. The form guides you through the steps.

We have included here a few of the earlier examples, redone using the new tables. Try a few if you care to see how it goes.

A Bit of History

The NAO tables were the invention of Admiral Thomas Davies and Dr. Paul Janiczek, then Head of the Astronomical Applications Department of the US Naval Observatory. They were originally published as the *Concise Tables for Sight Reduction* by Cornell Maritime Press. This type of table is referred to as "concise," or "compact," as opposed to the full form tables such as Pub 229 and 249, which are referred to as "inspection tables," since they require fewer steps.

Forerunners of these short tables were the Ageton Tables (Pub 211) and the Dreisenstock Tables (Pub 208). The Ageton Tables were included in Bowditch, Vol. 2 (editions prior to 1985) but not included in later editions, perhaps because they are now in the *Nautical Almanac*. Both Ageton and Dreisenstock are long out of print. US Power Squadron courses on celestial switched to the new NAO Tables shortly after they were published, with the help of US Power Squadron National Education Director Dr. Allan Bayless, who had published his own version of the tables called *Compact Sight Reduction Tables*.

Admiral Davies was aware of the Starpath work form (Form 106) for the NAO Tables and suggested at the time that it be included in the *Nautical Almanac*, which was agreed upon by the US NAO. The almanac, however, is a joint publication with the British NAO, and at the time they did not want to include any forms in the almanac, so this was dropped. In 2006, there was a change of heart in the UK, and a single-column work form now appears in the almanac for these tables. It is better than none, but it remains valuable to keep a Starpath form for these tables at hand; it takes you step by step through the process with no further instructions required.

Sight Reduction with the NAO Tables

The procedure used here is the same as presented in the Almanac, except for a change in notation explained below. In the work form, row numbers are marked with white numbers in black boxes. For Hs below 1° or above 87°, see special instructions at the end.

The angle notation used in the form is as follows:

$X = 35° 48'$ — an angle

$X° = 35°$ — degrees part of X

$X' = 48'$ — minutes part of X

$\overline{X} = 36°$ — X rounded to nearest whole degree.

Step 1. In the top lines of row 1, record assumed Latitude, LHA, and Declination (degrees in D°; minutes in D'). Circle the sign (+ or -) of D according to Same or Contrary name—or cross out the sign that does not apply.

Step 2. From the rules beside the Z_1 box, determine the sign of B and Z_1 (depends on LHA) and circle these signs in row 1 of the work form. B and Z_1 have the same sign.

Step 3. With LAT and LHA, enter the main Sight Reduction Table (SR Table on the form) and record A, B, and Z_1 in the spaces provided in row 1, separating degrees and minutes parts. Lat is found at the top of the Sight Reduction Tables; LHA on either side. Note the reminder of this arrangement at the top left of the form. This applies to all table entries.

Step 4. Copy A' to row 4 and circle the sign of C_2 according to the size of A'.

Step 5. Round off A to the nearest whole degree and record it as $\overline{A}$ in row 2.

Step 6. Sum D and B to get F, and record F° and F' in the spaces provided in row 1.

Step 7. From the size of F and the notes provided, determine the signs of Z_2 and C_1 and circle them in rows 2 and 3.

Step 8. Round off F to the nearest whole degree and record it as $\overline{F}$ in row 2.

Step 9. With $\overline{A}$ and $\overline{F}$, enter Sight Reduction Table and record H, P, and Z_2 into the spaces provided in row 2.

Step 10. Round off P and Z_2 to nearest whole degrees and record them as $\overline{P}$ and $\overline{Z_2}$ in rows 3 and 4.

Step 11. With F' and $\overline{P}$, enter the Auxiliary Table (Aux) and record C_1 in row 3. The Aux table is at the end of the Sight Reduction Table.

Step 12. With A' and $\overline{Z_2}$, enter the Auxiliary Table and record C_2 in row 4.

Step 13. Apply the corrections C_1 and C_2 (with their appropriate signs) to H to get Hc and record it in the space provided.

Step 14. Combine Z_1 and Z_2 (with their appropriate signs) to get Z and record it in the space provided. The result can be negative or positive (depending on the signs of Z_1 and Z_2), but this resulting sign is to be ignored—Z is to be treated as a positive number when later converting it to Zn.

Step 15. Record Ho in the space provided below Hc, then take their difference and record it as "a" in the space provided. Mark the proper label of the a-value using the rule if Hc is greater than Ho, then the label is "A," otherwise it is "T."

Step 16. Convert Z to Zn using the traditional rules located below the box for Z, and record the result in the space provided.

Step 17. Plot the LOP using the a-value, its label, and Zn

Low-altitude Sights (Hs below 1° or so)

For Hs values below 1° or so (sights that are usually only taken in desperation when other sights are not available), Ho, Hc, or both can be negative. In these cases, the Hs to Ho conversion must be done carefully, as signs can change as corrections are applied. Also, the procedure must be modified as follows: in Step 6 if F is negative (can only happen for very low sights), treat it as positive until the final Hc is determined in Step 13. And in Step 9, change Z_2 to $180°$ - Z_2 (remembering that the original Z_2 has a sign). In Step 13, if F was negative, change Hc to negative.

High-altitude Sights (Hs above 87° or so)

For very high sights, the standard plotting procedure of intersecting two straight LOPs does not provide a reliable fix, because these lines are no longer good approximations to the circles of position measured with the sextant. For high sights, it is best to plot the GP and then swing an arc from this point, using a radius equal to the zenith distance (90° - Ho). This arc is then a section of your circle of position.

It is difficult to estimate the errors caused by neglecting this procedure because they depend on the heights of all sights used for the fix. In any event, when a fix is made from data including a high sight, it is best to check this effect. Also, our preliminary study shows that the NAO type of Sight Reduction Table does not provide consistently accurate Zn values for very high sights. We have not analyzed this effect in detail. We have found no Zn problems for heights below 87°.

A compact set of Short Instructions are shown next along with two examples, Figure 106-1 and 106-2.

The NAO Tables are an excellent back up method, especially if you are relying on computed cel nav solutions routinely. With little practice, you will see process quickly, at which time it evolves from a complex solution to an elegant solution.

Form 106 Short Instructions

1. In row 1, record assumed Lat, LHA, and Dec (D). Mark the signs of D, B, and Z1.

2. In row 1, with Lat and LHA, enter Sight Reduction (SR) Table and record A, B, and Z1.

3. Add D and B to get F, and record it in row 1.

4. Copy A′ to row 4 and mark the sign of C2.

5. Round off A to nearest whole degree and record it as $\overline{A}$ in row 2.

6. Mark the signs of Z2 and C1 in rows 2 and 3.

7. Round off F to nearest whole degree and record it as $\overline{F}$ in row 2.

8. With $\overline{A}$ and $\overline{F}$, enter SR table and record H, P, and Z2 in row 2.

9. Round off P and Z2 to nearest whole degrees and record them as $\overline{P}$ and $\overline{Z2}$ in rows 3 and 4.

10. With F′ and $\overline{P}$, enter Auxiliary Table (Aux) and record C1 in row 3.

11. With A′ and $\overline{Z2}$, enter Aux table and record C2 in row 4.

12. Add C1 and C2 to H to get Hc.

13. Add Z1 and Z2 to get Z. Copy Z to space below it, rounding to nearest degree. Drop minus sign if present.

14. Convert Z to Zn by choosing appropriate Z sign next to LHA.

15. Record Ho below Hc; take their difference and record it as "a" with the proper label.

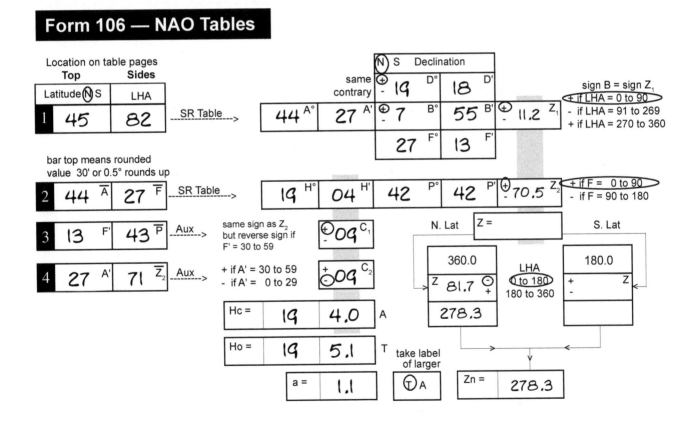

Figure 106-1. *Sight reduction using the NAO Sight Reduction Tables from the back of the Nautical Almanac and Form 106. The starting data are: Lat 45°, Dec 19° 18' Same Name, and LHA 82°. The bottom part of the form is for the corrected sextant measurement (Ho) and altitude intercept (a-value) computation, along with final azimuth computation which are need to plot the line of position. The exact values from direct computation are Hc = 19° 3.7' and Zn = 278.6°. The Ho value used to compute the altitude intercept (a) comes from a different form. Form 106 provides only the Hc and Zn values. See Figure 108-1.*

Form 106 — NAO Tables

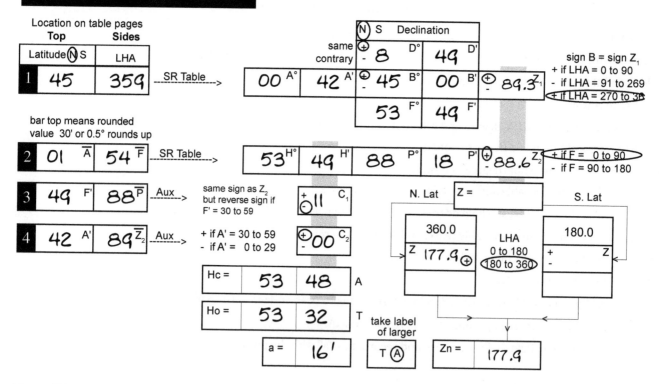

Figure 106-2. *Sight reduction using the NAO Sight Reduction Tables from the back of the Nautical Almanac and Form 106. The starting data are: Lat 45°, Dec 8° 49' Same Name, and LHA 359°. The bottom part of the form is for the corrected sextant measurement (Ho) and altitude intercept (a-value) computation, along with final azimuth computation which are needed to plot the line of position. The exact values from direct computation are Hc = 53° 48.4' and Zn = 178.3°.*

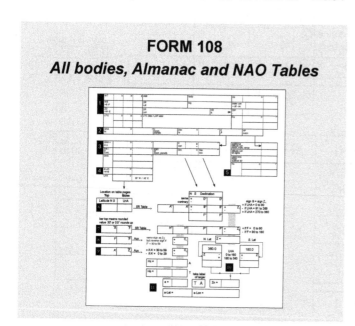

FORM 108
All bodies, Almanac and NAO Tables

Form 108 Short Instructions

(1) Fill in sight data.

(2) Get GHA and declination (Dec) data from Daily Pages for whole hour.

(3) Get minutes and seconds corrections. Sum for GHA, Sum for Dec. Copy Dec to line in 6. Mark N or S.

(4) Choose a-Lon and find LHA. Copy to line (6). Choose a-Lat, record in line (5). Record a-Lat and a-Lon in line (11).

(5) Apply altitude corrections to get Ho. Copy Ho to space above (11).

(6) to (10) Follow standard NAO Form 106 instructions.

(11) Find a-value as difference between Hc and Ho, and choose its label. Now all data needed to plot the LOP is at hand.

Form 108 for Almanac and NAO Tables

This convenient form combines use of the *Nautical Almanac* and Form 104 with the sight reduction using NAO Tables and Form 106. An example is in Figure 108-1. Instructions for the top part are found in the Form 104 section, and those for the bottom part are presented in the Form 106 section.

Form 108 — Almanac + NAO Tables

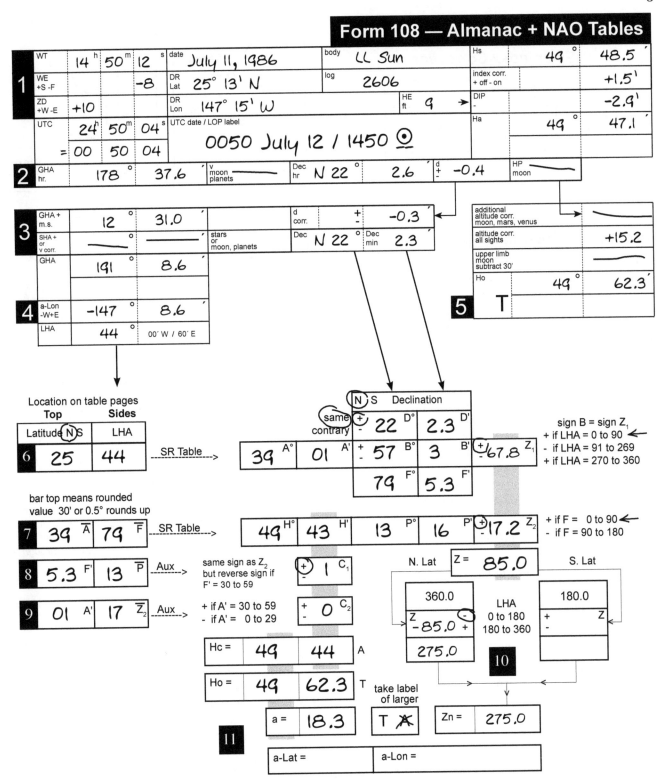

Figure 108-1. *Form 108 is a combination of Form 104 (top part) for the Almanac look up data and Form 106, which is used for the NAO Tables sight reduction (bottom part). This example uses data from Figure 104-1, which yields Pub 249 values of Hc = 49° 43.3' (after interpolation of the d correction) at Zn = 275. The NAO Tables get 49° 44' at Zn = 275.0. These are to be compared to the more precise values obtained by computation of 49° 43.2' at Zn = 275.2. This Hc discrepancy of 0.8' is about as large as will ever be seen in the use of the NAO Tables.*

FORM 109
Solar Index Correction

Toward or Away		Date			
On	Off	Diff		Check SD	
sight #	-	-		+	
	=	=	÷2	=	÷4
SD=		=		=	

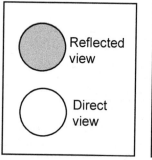

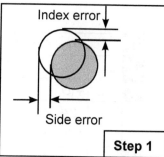

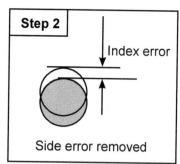

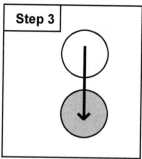

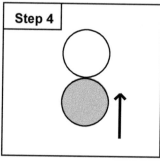

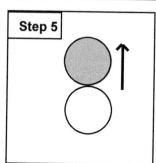

Figure 109-1. *Views through the sextant during a solar IC measurement. The gray sun is the reflected view seen on the right side of the horizon mirror; the white sun is the direct view through the clear glass of the left side of the horizon glass.*

Form 109 for Solar Index Correction

This method of measuring the index correction dates to one of the first definitive texts on cel nav from the late 1700s. It has the advantage over the standard use of the sea horizon in that it provides a self consistency check on the results with a measurement of the semidiameter (SD) of the sun that is listed in the Almanac. On the other hand, this measurement is a rare example of when cel nav can be dangerous!

CAUTION!

You will be looking straight toward the sun for this method through a telescope. So you must be certain that all sun shades are in place and you do not somehow distort your view and look around the edge of the shades. *Do not under any circumstances look directly at the sun with or without a telescope unless there are proper shades in place.* We recommend that you read our article on this procedure before using it.

starpath.com/solar_method

That article also shows how to build a custom sun filter for the end of the telescope as well as how to add a protective mask around the telescope to prevent an inadvertent glance past the main sun shade.

Procedure

Use the highest power scope you have for this. A 7 x 35 monocular is best if you have one. If not using a custom sun filter, adjust the sextant shades so the reflected and direct view of the sun appear as different colors. A dedicated telescope sun filter makes both views the same color, with just brightness differing.

(Step 1) With all shades in place, set the sextant to 0° 0.0' and look toward the sun on a clear day. You will see something like that shown in Step 1 of Figure 109-1.

(Step 2) Use standard sextant adjustment procedures to remove the side error to yield the view shown in Step 2.

We now need to specify a rotation direction for the micrometer drum, as we hold the sextant in our right hand and turn the micrometer with our left hand as we look down on it with the sextant frame parallel to the ground. We use the label *toward* for a clockwise rotation and *away* for counterclockwise. The terms come from viewing the drum as you turn it. The *toward* rotation (clockwise) brings the numbers on the top of the dial toward you as they decrease in value. *Away* means the opposite: a counterclockwise turn, with numbers increasing as the they move away from you. Needless to say, this is just a notation that has proven useful to us. Others may prefer different notations, in which case change the form label "Toward" to "CW" and "Away" to "CCW." Any method to keep track of the direction you are turning the drum will do.

The key point is that in essentially all sextants the values of the IC that you get when done carefully depends on the direction you rotate to achieve final alignment. This is not necessarily a mechanical property of the sextant; it is a combination of sextant plus human perception of alignment. On *most* metal sextants this is a much smaller effect than it is on *all* plastic sextants.

First we measure the "Toward" value of the IC.

(Step 3) Turn the micrometer away from you until all of the reflected image is well below the direct image.

(Step 4) Now turn micrometer toward you slowly and uniformly so that the reflected image rises until the top edge of it just touches the bottom edge of the direct image. And then read the dial. It should read something around 32' (2 x SD) on the scale—depending on your IC. Record this ON value, accurate to the tenth. In example 1 we measured 34.0' ON. There is a form showing this example and several others in Figure 109-2.

(Step 5) Now continue to turn, slowly and uniformly, in the toward direction until the bottom edge of the reflected image aligns with the top edge of the direct image. If we overshoot we need to start all over again! The idea is to be turning in only one direction when we stop. This time the dial will read about 28' but this will be an OFF the scale measurement, so we have to subtract whatever it reads from 60. In this example the micrometer read 29.2', which would be 60.0'-29.2' = 30.8' OFF the scale. Record this OFF value.

(Step 6) Now take the difference between the ON value and the OFF value and divide that by 2 to find your IC. Just subtract the smaller from the larger. The label of your result will be the same as the label of the larger value. In this example: 34.0 - 30.8 = 3.2' and 3.2'/2 = 1.6' and since 34 was ON, the answer is ON, i.e., our IC is 1.6' ON the scale.

(Step 7) Now check your result by comparing to the actual semidiameter (SD) of the sun at the time of the sight. Our example was measured on 02/28/01 using an Astra IIIB deluxe model sextant with traditional mirror. From the *Nautical Almanac*, we get that SD = 16.2'. The SD of the sun equals the ON value plus the OFF value divided by 4. In this example, 34.0+30.8 = 64.8 and 64.8/4 = 16.2 which is right.

Then repeat the full process turning always in the Away direction to get the "Away" value of the IC. Careful measurements usually show a slight difference for the Toward and Away values, even for a high quality metal sextant. For plastic sextants, on the other hand, the difference between toward and away values will almost always be rather large, some few minutes or so.

Another Check

A quick method to measure the IC this way, or maybe to double-check the result to see that it all makes sense, is just to align the reflected and direct images on top of each other and read the dial. That reading will be your IC, but the above procedure is a more accurate way to get the value. In this case we would see what is shown here, depending on whether or not we had side error. In our example, the dial would read 1.6' ON the scale when either of the two right-side alignments were set.

For Best Results

Because an important part of this method is that it includes a measurement of the sun's SD, choose a sun height above 20° or so to reduce uncertainty from refraction when comparing your measured SD with the actual SD. At low heights the refraction is changing fast with angle. At 5°, for example, this would cause an error of about 0.8', and worse lower. At 10° this error is down to 0.3' and it is essentially gone at 30° and higher. An outstretched hand span held vertical (tip of little finger to tip of thumb) is roughly 30° on many hands.

Form 109 — Solar IC

Date ___2/28/01___ SD ___16.2'___
[Toward] or Away

ON	OFF	Diff	Check SD
34.0	60.0	34.0	34.0
1. −29.2	−30.8	+30.8	+30.8
= 30.8	= 3.2 ÷2	= 64.8 ÷4	
	= 1.6 on	= 16.2	

ON	OFF	Diff	Check SD
33.8	60.0	33.8	33.8
2. −29.8	−30.2	+30.2	
= 30.2	= 3.6 ÷2	= 64.0 ÷4	
	= 1.8 on	= 16.0	

Date ___2/28/01___ SD ___16.2'___
Toward or [Away]

ON	OFF	Diff	CheckSD
33.6	60.0	33.6	33.6
1. −28.8	−31.2	+31.2	
= 31.2	= 2.4 ÷2	= 64.8 ÷4	
	= 1.2 on	= 16.2	

ON	OFF	Diff	Check SD
33.4	60.0	33.4	33.4
2. −29.0	−31.0	+31.0	
= 31.0	= 2.4 ÷2	= 64.4 ÷4	
	= 1.2	= 16.1	

Figure 109-2. *A section of Form 109 used to evaluate the Index Correction measured from the sun. The normal procedure is to make multiple measurements and then average them. The full form has places for 12 of these measurements.*

FORM 107
Latitude at LAN

Step 1   Correct Hs to get Ho

1-1	Record Maximum Sextant Height (Hs = peak height of the sun at noon), and mark limb	Lower / Upper	Hs	° ′
1-2	Record Index Correction (mark sign = if off, - if on)	IC	Off + / On −	′
1-3	Record eye height (HE) and Look up Dip Correction on the right-hand side of Table A2, front of the Almanac (correction depends on HE)	HE Ø ø	Dip −	′
1-4	Sum the above three numbers to get Apparent Height		Ha	° ′
1-5	Look up altitude correction on left-hand side of Table A2, front of the Almanac (correction depends on Ha, Limb, and month) (mark sign = for lower limb, - for upper limb)		Alt corr.	+ / − ′
1-6	Sum the above two numbers to get Observed Height		Ho	° ′

Step 2   Determine the Zenith Distance   89° 60.0′

2-1	Record Ho from Step 1 above, and then subtract it from 90° to get the zenith distance	Ho	° − ′
2-2	Zenith distance		

Step 3   Use the Almanac to Find Sun's Declination   GMT date =

3-1	Record the date and GMT of the sight (the time the sun reached its peak height)	GMT (hr) =	GMT (min) =	
3-2	Turn to the daily page of the Almanac for the date of the sight, and find the sun's declination (dec) for the hour of the sight (line 3-1) and record it here.	Dec (hr) =	N / S	
3-3	Record the d-value from the bottom of the dec column in the Almanac. Mark the signs of the d-value and d-corr = if the dec for the next hour is larger, or − if it is smaller.	d-value = + / −	d-corr = + / −	
3-4	Turn to the Increments and Corrections pages at the back of the Almanac (1-9 to 12), in the noted and find the minutes table for the GMT minutes (line 3-1). On the right-hand side of the double line in the table, find the d-corr corresponding to the d-value of line 3-3.	3-5	Apply the d-corr to the dec(hr) and record it above.	Declination = N / S ° ′

Step 4   Find Latitude from Zenith Distance and Declination

Record DR Latitude to use as a guide, and then take the sum or difference of zenith distance and declination to find your true Latitude at LAN.

Declination or Zenith distance	° ′
Zenith distance or Declination	° ′
Latitude =	° ′

FORM 110
Latitude by Polaris

Step 1. Correct Hs to get Ho

1-1	Record Sextant Height of *Polaris*	Hs	° ′
1-2	Record Index Correction *"If it's off, put it on; if it's on, take it off."*		Off + / On − ′
1-3	Record height of eye (HE=____) and look up Dip Correction on the right-hand side of Table A2, front of Almanac		Dip − ′
1-4	Sum the above to get the Apparent Height of *Polaris*	Ha	° ′
1-5	Look up the Altitude Correction (always minus)	alt corr.	− ′
1-6	Sum the above two numbers to get Observed Height	Ho	° ′

Step 2. Find LHA Aries (ϒ)   UTC Date =

2-1	UTC Time in Hours, Minutes and Seconds	UTC Time =	
2-2	Find GHA ϒ on left-hand side of daily pages of the Nautical Almanac	GHA ϒ (hr) =	° ′
2-3	Find GHA Aries minutes and seconds correction from Increments and Corrections pages	GHA ϒ (m, s) =	′
2-4	Sum the above two numbers to get GHA Aries	GHA ϒ =	° ′
	Extra spaces to adjust angles as needed		
2-5	DR Lon: −West; +East	−W, +E	° ′
2-6	Combine 2-4 and 2-5 to get LHA ϒ	LHA ϒ =	° ′

Step 3. Latitude Determination

3-1	Ho from 1-6	Ho	° ′
3-2	Subtract 1°		−1°
3-3	Add a0 from *Polaris* Table (using LHA Aries)	+a0	′
3-4	Add a1 from *Polaris* Table (using DR Latitude)	+a1	′
3-5	Add a2 from *Polaris* Table (using Month)	+a2	′
3-6	Sum the above to find Latitude	Latitude =	° ′

Note that this procedure for finding Lat from Polaris is explained in the Nautical Almanac.

FORM 117
Lat, Lon at LAN plus Polaris

Lat at LAN	degrees	minutes
Find Ho		
Hs-max =		
IC (+Off, − On) = ±		
Dip (from HE) = −		
Ha =		
alt corr (+LL,−UL) = ±		
Ho =		
Find z (90°-Ho)	89°	60.0′
Ho =		
z =		
DR (Lat, Lon) =		
Lat = sum or difference Dec and z		
Dec or z =		
z or Dec = ±		
Lat =		

Date	hr	min	sec
UTC LAN =			

Declination in Nautical Almanac at UTC of LAN	degrees	minutes	d-value (s)
Dec (hr) = N S			
d corr = ±			
Dec = N S			

Lon at LAN = GHA sun at UTC of LAN	degrees	minutes
GHA (hr) =		
GHA (m,s) = +		
GHA =		
If GHA between 0 and 180, Lon W = GHA		
If GHA between 180 and 360, Lon E = 360−GHA		

LAN Lat Rules: For Contrary Name: Lat = z − Dec. For Same Name: DR-Lat > Dec, Lat = z + Dec; DR-Lat < Dec, Lat = Dec − z. But don't forget the easy rule: add them, and if that is nonsense (compared to your DR Lat) then sub-tract them. **LAN Lon Reminder:** LAN Lon is only as accurate as the UTC you assign to the event. The Lon will be uncertain by 15′ for each 1 minute of time uncertainty in your choice of peak Hs time.

Find LHA ϒ	hr	min	sec
UTC *Polaris* sight			
Date			
DR (Lat, Lon) =			
	degrees	minutes	
LHA ϒ = GHA ϒ − Lon W (or + Lon E)			
GHA ϒ (hr) =			
GHA ϒ (m,s) = +			
GHA ϒ =			
DR Lon (−W,+E) = ±			
LHA ϒ =			

Use LHA ϒ in Polaris Tables to find a0, a1, a2

Lat by Polaris	degrees	minutes
Hs of *Polaris* =		
IC (+Off, −On) = ±		
Dip (from HE) = −		
Ha =		
alt corr = −		
Ho =		
subtract 1° = −1°		
+a0 = +		
+a1 = +		
+a2 = +		
Lat =		

Forms 107, 110, and 117 for Noon Sights and *Polaris* Sights

This set of forms differ from the others in that Form 107 and Form 110 incorporate detailed instructions right in the forms themselves, whereas Form 117 combines both of these and has no separate instructions.

The procedures covered in these forms have few steps and are sights covered early in cel nav training. After working a few examples using the annotated forms, the process is typically understood and easy to follow, which leaves only the need for a form (117) that offers places to put the values for easy organization and arithmetic.

Latitude at LAN (local apparent noon) is a way to find latitude from the peak height of the sun at noon; latitude by Polaris is an analogous short procedure for finding latitude from the height of *Polaris*. Both require only the *Nautical Almanac*.

Form 117 adds to the noon sight the ability to find longitude from the time of the peak height. The solution is very easy but finding the time of the peak height takes special sights.

Figure 107-1 shows a Lat by LAN sight worked out. Figure 110-1 shows a *Polaris* sight worked out, and Figure 117-1 shows how these data would be presented in that form along with the extra step of solving for longitude.

Form 107— Lat by *Polaris*

Step 1 Correct Hs to get Ho

1-1	Record Maximum Sextant Height (Hs = peak height of the sun at noon), and mark limb	(Lower) / Upper	Hs	74°	57.2'
1-2	Record Index Correction (mark sign + if off, - if on)	IC	Off ⊕ / On −		1.3'
1-3	Record eye height (HE) and Look up Dip Correction on the right-hand side of Table A2, front of the Almanac (correction depends on HE) — HE (ft) 9 ft	Dip	⊖		2.9'
1-4	Sum the above three numbers to get Apparent Height	Ha		74°	55.6'
1-5	Look up altitude correction on lefthand side of Table A2, front of the Almanac (correction depends on Ha, Limb, and month) (mark sign + for lower limb, - for upper limb)	Alt corr.	⊕ / ⊖		15.7'
1-6	Sum the above two numbers to get Observed Height	Ho		74°	71.3'

Step 2 Determine the Zenith Distance

			89°	60.0'
2-1	Record Ho from Step 1, above, and then subtract it from 90° to get the zenith distance	Ho	− 75°	11.3'
2-2	Zenith distance	z	14°	48.7'

Step 3 Use the Almanac to Find Sun's Declination

GMT date = Jul 14, 2018

3-1	Record the date and GMT of the sight (the time the sun reached its peak height)	GMT (hr) = 20 h	GMT (min) = 49 m
3-2	Turn to the daily page of the Almanac for the date of the sight, and find the sun's declination (dec) for the hour of the sight (line 3-1) and record it here.	Dec (hr)	(N)/S 21° 35.2'
3-3	Record the d-value from the bottom of the dec column in the Almanac. Mark the signs of the d-value and d-corr + if the dec for the next hour is larger, or - if it is smaller.	d-value = + / ⊖ 0.4	d-corr = ⊕ / − 0.3'
3-4	Turn to the Increments and Corrections pages at the back of the Almanac (T-9 to 12, in the notes) and find the minutes table for the GMT minutes (line 3-1). On the right-hand side of the double line in the table, find the d-corr corresponding to the d-value of line 3-3.	Declination =	N/S 21° 34.9'
		3-5 Apply the d-corr to the dec(hr) and record it above.	

Step 4 Find Latitude from Zenith Distance and Declination

Record DR Latitude to use as a guide, and then take the sum or difference of zenith distance and declination to find your true Latitude at LAN.

Declination or Zenith distance	21°	34.9'
Zenith distance or Declination	14°	48.7'
Latitude =	35°	83.6'

= 36° 23.6'

Figure 107-1. *A noon sight for latitude solved using Form 107. After some practice, the shorter Form 117 can be used.*

Form 110 — Lat from *Polaris*

	Step 1. Correct Hs to get Ho				
1-1	Record Sextant Height of *Polaris*		Hs	49 °	34.0'
1-2	Record Index Correction *"If it's off, put it on; if it's on, take it off."*		Off ⊕ On −		1.3 '
1-3	Record height of eye (HE=____) and look up Dip Correction on the right-hand side of Table A2, front of Almanac		Dip −		2.9 '
1-4	Sum the above to get the Apparent Height of *Polaris*		Ha	49 °	32.4'
1-5	Look up the Altitude Correction (always minus)		alt corr.	−	0.8'
1-6	Sum the above two numbers to get Observed Height		Ho	49 °	31.6'

	Step 2. Find LHA Aries (♈)	UTC Date =	Apr 21, 2018		
2-1	UTC Time in Hours, Minutes and Seconds	UTC Time =	23	18	56
2-2	Find GHA ♈ on left-hand side of daily pages of the Nautical Almanac	GHA ♈ (hr) =	194°		57.7 '
2-3	Find GHA Aries minutes and seconds correction from Increments and Corrections pages	GHA ♈ (m, s) =	4°		44.8'
2-4	Sum the above two numbers to get GHA Aries	GHA ♈ =	198°		102.5'
	Extra spaces to adjust angles as needed		199		42.5
2-5	DR Lon: −West; +East	⊖W +E	−37°		14.0'
2-6	Combine 2-4 and 2-5 to get LHA ♈	LHA ♈ =	162 °		28.5 '

	Step 3. Latitude Determination				
3-1	Ho from 1-6		Ho	49 °	31.6'
3-2	Subtract 1°			−1 °	
3-3	Add a0 from *Polaris* Table (using LHA Aries)		+a0	1°	18.0
3-4	Add a1 from *Polaris* Table (using DR Latitude)		+a1		0.6'
3-5	Add a2 from *Polaris* Table (using Month)		+a2		0.9'
3-6	Sum the above to find Latitude		Latitude =	49 °	51.1'

Note that this procedure for finding Lat from Polaris is explained in the Nautical Almanac.

Figure 110-1. *Finding latitude from a Polaris sight using Form 110.*

Form 117 — LAN and *Polaris* Sights

Lat at LAN			
Find Ho		degrees	minutes
Hs-max =		74	57.2
IC (+Off, - On) =	±		+1.3
Dip (from HE) =	−		-2.9
Ha =		74	55.6
alt corr (UL-(LL+)) =	±		+15.7
Ho =		74	71.3
		= 75	11.3
Find z (90°-Ho)		89°	60.0'
Ho =	−	-75	11.3
z =		14	48.7
DR (Lat, Lon) =		36°31' N, 130°15' W	
Lat = sum or difference Dec and z			
~~Dec or~~ z =		14	48.7
~~z or~~ Dec =	±	21	34.9
Lat =		35	83.6
		=36°	23.6'

Date Jul 14, 2018		hr	min	sec
UTC LAN =		20	48	35

Declination in Nautical Almanac at UTC of LAN				
		degrees	minutes	d-value (±)
Dec (hr) = (N) S		21	35.2	-0.4
d corr =	±		-0.3	
Dec = (N) S		21	34.9	

Lon at LAN = GHA sun at UTC of LAN			
		degrees	minutes
GHA (hr) =		118	31.2
GHA (m.s) =	+	12	8.8
GHA =		130	40.0
If GHA between 0 and 180, Lon W = GHA			
If GHA between 180 and 360, Lon E = 360-GHA			

LAN Lat Rules: *For Contrary Name: Lat = z - Dec. For Same Name: DR-Lat > Dec, Lat = z + Dec; DR-Lat < Dec, Lat = Dec -z. But don't forget the easy rule: add them, and if that is nonsense (compared to your DR Lat) then sub-tract them.* **LAN Lon Reminder:** *LAN Lon is only as accurate as the UTC you assign to the event. The Lon will be uncertain by 15' for each 1 minute of time uncertainty in your choice of peak Hs time.*

Find LHA ♈			
UTC *Polaris* sight	hr	min	sec
Date Apr 21, 2018	23	18	56
DR (Lat, Lon) =	49°50' N, 37°14' W		

LHA ♈ = GHA ♈ - Lon W (or + Lon E)			
		degrees	minutes
GHA ♈ (hr) =		194	57.7
GHA ♈ (m.s) =	+	4	44.8
GHA ♈ =		198	102.5
		199	42.5
DR Lon (-W,+E) =	±	-37	14.0
LHA ♈ =		162	28.5
Use LHA ♈ in Polaris Tables to find a0, a1, a2			

Lat by *Polaris*			
		degrees	minutes
Hs of *Polaris* =		49	34.0
IC (+Off, - On) =	±		+1.3
Dip (from HE) =	−		-2.9
Ha =		49	32.4
alt corr =	−		-0.8
Ho =		49	31.6
subtract 1°	−	-1°	
+a0 =	+	1	18.0
+a1 =	+		0.6
+a2 =	+		0.9
Lat =		49	51.1

Figure 117-1. *The short form that combines Form 107 and Form 110. The example here are data from Figures 107-1 and 110-1.*

FORM 111
Pub 249, Vol. 1 Selected Stars

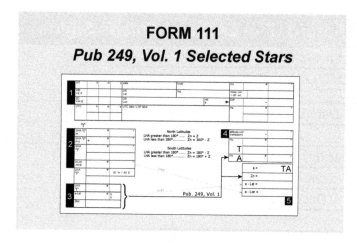

Form 111 Star Sight Reduction with Pub 249 Vol. 1, Selected Stars

Pub 249 Sight Reduction tables come in three volumes. Vols. 2 and 3 are meant for sun, moon, and planets and thus only cover declinations (dec) under 29°. Vol. 2 is for observing latitudes of 0° to 40°; Vol. 3 is for latitudes of 39° to 89°. We can use it for stars, providing they have dec <29°, which would be the ones circling the earth over the subtropical belt of the earth. These two volumes are permanent publications, just as Pub 229, that apply to any year.

Pub 249 Vol. 1, on the other hand, is unique in this set, as it applies to any latitude, but only covers selected stars. It is also unique in providing Hc and Zn directly for each of the selected stars at specific times and latitudes, as well as recommending which triad of stars offers the best fix, based on relative bearings, altitudes, and brightness. Because it is so specific, it must be recomputed every 5 years, labeled by the valid Epoch year, with the data being valid for the 2 years before and after the Epoch year.

Pub 249 Vol. 1 can be used to predict the best 3 stars to use for a star-only fix and also then used as a way to sight reduce these stars to get the 2 LOPs for a fix. It does not take into account the use of planets, so it will likely miss the truly best triad of sights when Venus or Jupiter are in view at sight time. However, we know from Vols. 2 or 3 the bearings and heights of the planets so we can figure the best sights on our own in these cases.

Form 111 is designed to accommodate the unique sight reduction procedure that is used with Vol. 1. The instructions that follow apply to the sight reduction itself once the sight has been taken. But users will find that if Vol.1 has been used to predict the best stars, then most of the data needed will already be at hand. In short, an advantage of this method is that usually the very process of predicting the best stars completes most of the sight reduction. On the other hand, even if just used for sight reduction, the process is much faster than other methods.

In the instructions that follow, we look at the Vol. 1 method using Form 111 compared to the same sight reduction using Vol. 2 and Form 104. The results look a bit different in the two forms, but they yield the same LOP as shown in Figure 111-1.

Instructions for Sight Reduction with Pub 249, Vol. 1

Box 1. This is the raw sight data and time corrections covered in the instructions to Form 104.

Box 2. Use the almanac to find GHA of Aries at the UTC of the sight. Choose an assumed Lon in the normal manner (see Form 104 instructions). And then find local hour angle of Aries in the normal manner. Copy a-Lon to Box 5 for later use in plotting.

Box 3. Enter star name, and LHA Aries from Box 2, and enter an assumed Lat equal to actual DR-Lat rounded to nearest whole degree. Box 3 now contains all we need to enter Pub 249 Vol. 1. Copy a-Lat to Box 5 for later use in plotting.

Inside Pub 249 Vol. 1, find the right Lat on the top corners of the pages, go to your star column and down to the corresponding LHA Aries. Copy the Hc to Box 4 and Zn to Box 5. (This step takes seconds; there are no corrections as when using other methods.)

Box 4. Correct Hs to get Ho in the normal manner using the star altitude correction from *Nautical Almanac*.

Box 5. Find the difference between Hc and Ho, which is the altitude intercept (a). Give it the label T or A depending on which is larger in Box 4. Now Box 5 contains all the information we need to plot the LOP.

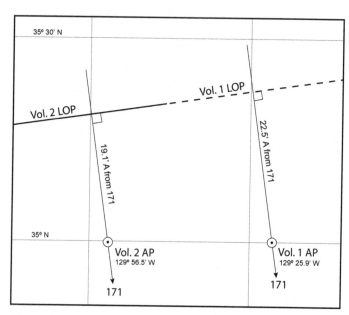

Figure 111-1. *Plots of the two LOPs from Figure 111-2. Since the procedures call for different assumed longitudes, we cannot compare the final a-values, but once plotted we do indeed get the same LOPs. The Vol. 1 method is fast, but it calls for a different procedure for these sights. If we use Pub 229 or the NAO Tables, then all sights are worked the same way, which has some virtue.*

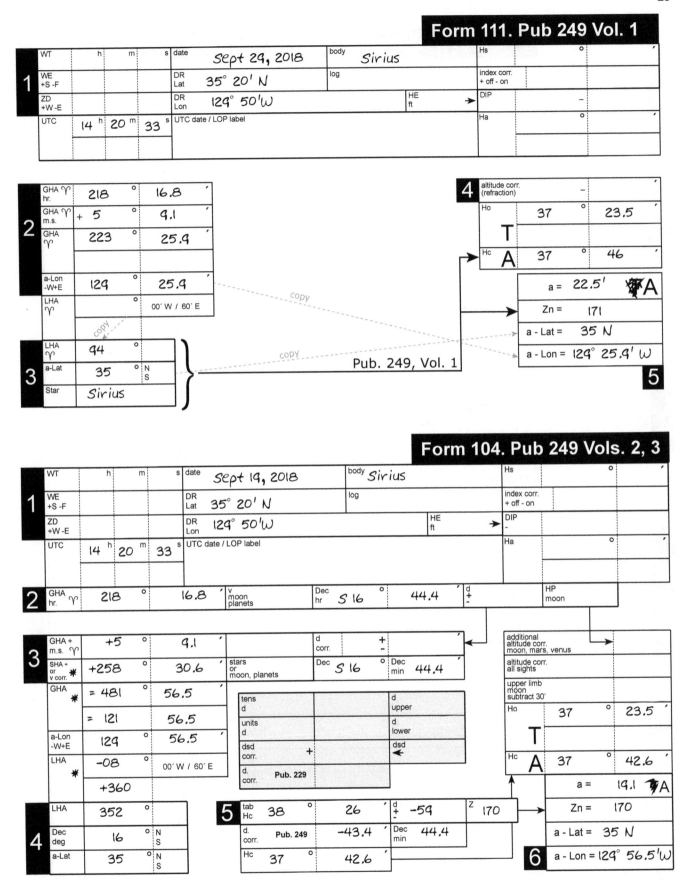

Figure 111-2. *The top shows the sight reduction of a selected star from Pub 249 Vol. 1 using Form 111. The bottom part is the same star sight reduced with Pub 249 Vol. 2 using Form 104. The Vol. 1 solution is much faster and yields equivalent results (Figure 111-1), but only applies to the specific Selected Stars listed in Vol. 1. Vols. 2 and 3 can only be used with star declinations <29°.*

Form 104, All Sights, Pub. 249 or Pub. 229

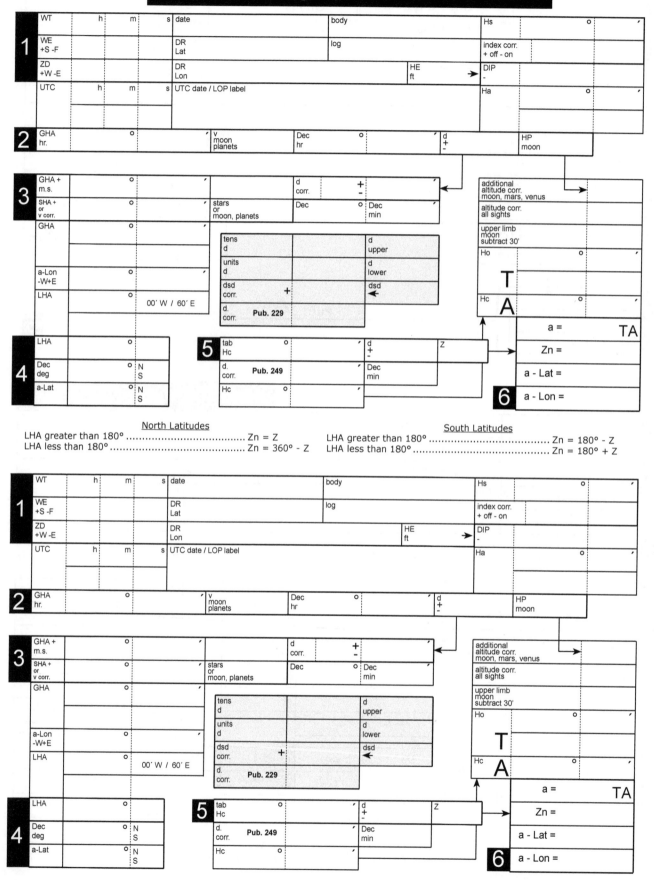

North Latitudes

LHA greater than 180° .... Zn = Z

LHA less than 180° .... Zn = 360° - Z

South Latitudes

LHA greater than 180° .... Zn = 180° - Z

LHA less than 180° .... Zn = 180° + Z

Form 104, All Sights, Pub. 249 or Pub. 229

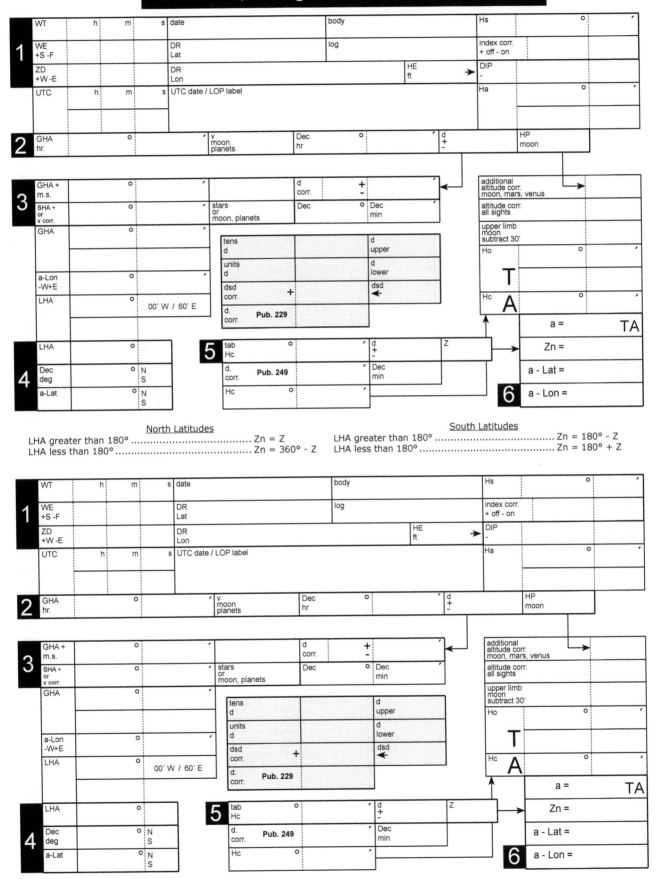

North Latitudes

LHA greater than 180° .... Zn = Z

LHA less than 180° .... Zn = 360° - Z

South Latitudes

LHA greater than 180° .... Zn = 180° - Z

LHA less than 180° .... Zn = 180° + Z

Form 104, All Sights, Pub. 249 or Pub. 229

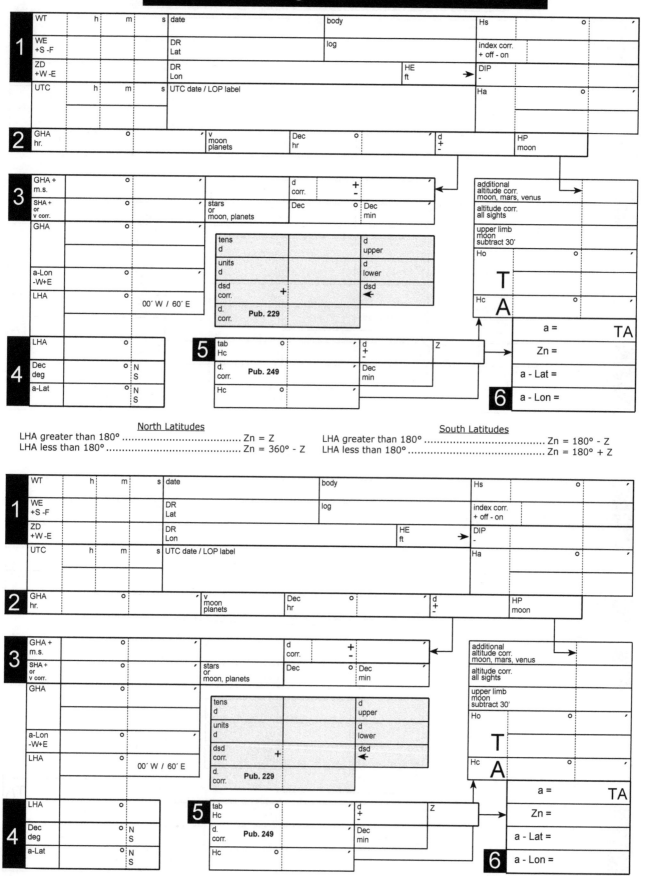

North Latitudes

LHA greater than 180° .... Zn = Z
LHA less than 180° .... Zn = 360° - Z

South Latitudes

LHA greater than 180° .... Zn = 180° - Z
LHA less than 180° .... Zn = 180° + Z

Form 104, All Sights, Pub. 249 or Pub. 229

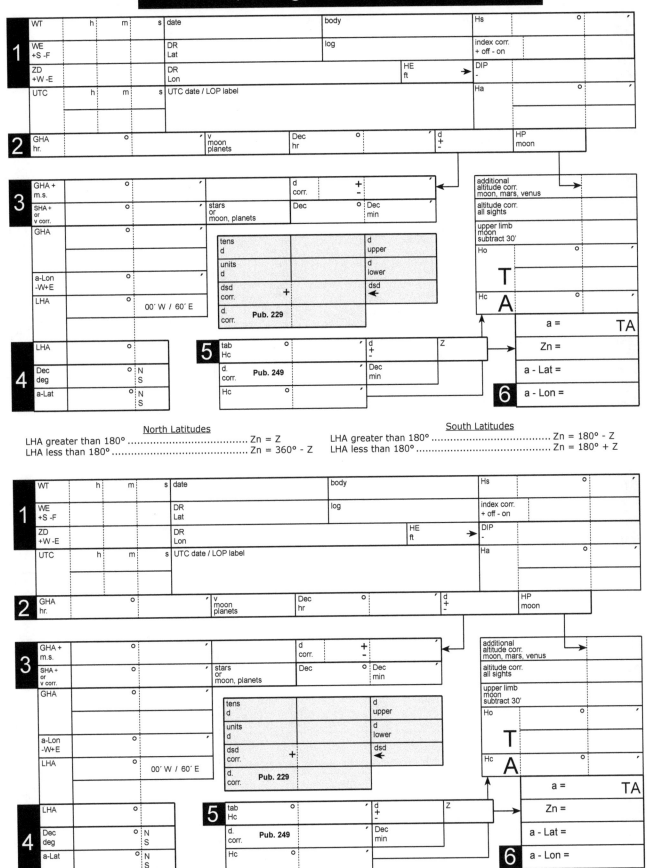

North Latitudes

LHA greater than 180° .... Zn = Z
LHA less than 180° .... Zn = 360° - Z

South Latitudes

LHA greater than 180° .... Zn = 180° - Z
LHA less than 180° .... Zn = 180° + Z

Form 104, All Sights, Pub. 249 or Pub. 229

1

WT	h	m	s	date		body		Hs		°		′
WE +S -F				DR Lat		log		index corr. + off - on				
ZD +W -E				DR Lon			HE ft →	DIP -				
UTC	h	m	s	UTC date / LOP label				Ha		°		′

2

| GHA hr. | | ° | | ′ | v moon planets | Dec hr | ° | ′ | d + - | | HP moon | |

3

GHA + m.s.		°		′		d corr.		+ -		′		additional altitude corr. moon, mars, venus
SHA + or v corr.		°		′	stars or moon, planets	Dec	°	Dec min				altitude corr. all sights
GHA		°		′								upper limb moon subtract 30′

tens d / units d / dsd corr. + / d. corr. **Pub. 229** — d upper / d lower / dsd ←

| a-Lon -W+E | | ° | | ′ | | | | | | | | Ho | | ° | | ′ |
| LHA | | ° | | ′ | 00′ W / 60′ E | | | | | | | | Hc | | ° | | ′ |

T A

4

LHA		°	
Dec deg		°	N S
a-Lat		°	N S

5

tab Hc		°		′	d +	Dec min	Z	
d. corr. **Pub. 249**								
Hc		°		′				

6

a =		TA
Zn =		
a - Lat =		
a - Lon =		

North Latitudes		South Latitudes	
LHA greater than 180° .... Zn = Z		LHA greater than 180° .... Zn = 180° - Z	
LHA less than 180° .... Zn = 360° - Z		LHA less than 180° .... Zn = 180° + Z	

1

WT	h	m	s	date		body		Hs		°		′
WE +S -F				DR Lat		log		index corr. + off - on				
ZD +W -E				DR Lon			HE ft →	DIP -				
UTC	h	m	s	UTC date / LOP label				Ha		°		′

2

| GHA hr. | | ° | | ′ | v moon planets | Dec hr | ° | ′ | d + - | | HP moon | |

3

GHA + m.s.		°		′		d corr.		+ -		′		additional altitude corr. moon, mars, venus
SHA + or v corr.		°		′	stars or moon, planets	Dec	°	Dec min				altitude corr. all sights
GHA		°		′								upper limb moon subtract 30′

tens d / units d / dsd corr. + / d. corr. **Pub. 229** — d upper / d lower / dsd ←

| a-Lon -W+E | | ° | | ′ | | | | | | | | Ho | | ° | | ′ |
| LHA | | ° | | ′ | 00′ W / 60′ E | | | | | | | | Hc | | ° | | ′ |

T A

4

LHA		°	
Dec deg		°	N S
a-Lat		°	N S

5

tab Hc		°		′	d +	Dec min	Z	
d. corr. **Pub. 249**								
Hc		°		′				

6

a =		TA
Zn =		
a - Lat =		
a - Lon =		

27

Form 104, All Sights, Pub. 249 or Pub. 229

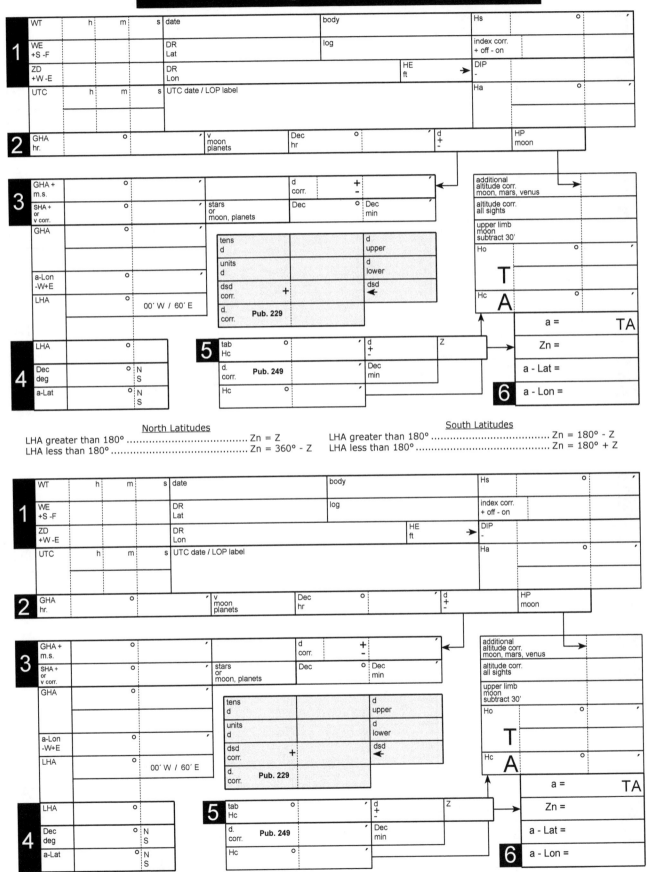

North Latitudes
LHA greater than 180° .... Zn = Z
LHA less than 180° .... Zn = 360° - Z

South Latitudes
LHA greater than 180° .... Zn = 180° - Z
LHA less than 180° .... Zn = 180° + Z

Form 104, All Sights, Pub. 249 or Pub. 229

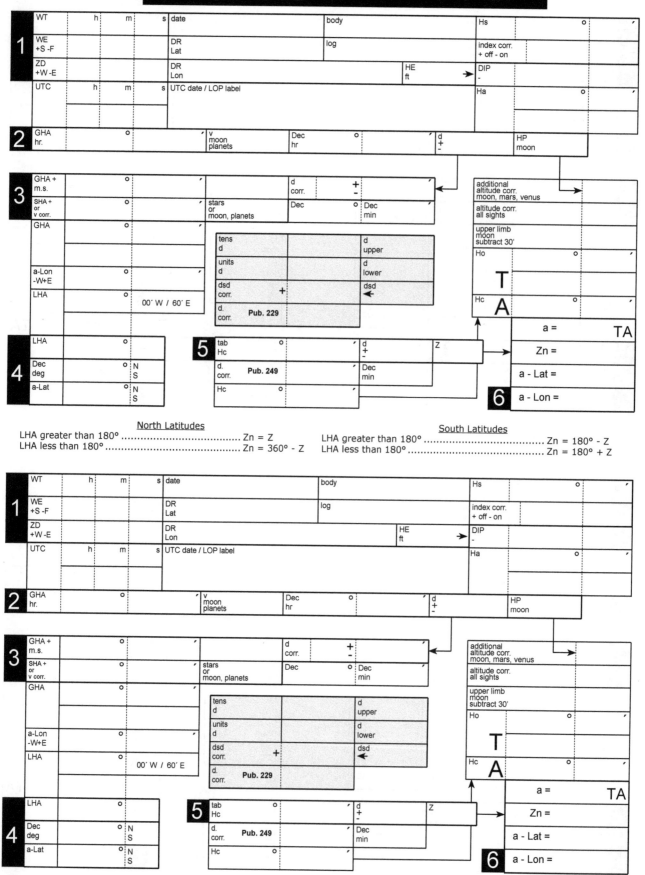

North Latitudes

LHA greater than 180° .... Zn = Z
LHA less than 180° .... Zn = 360° - Z

South Latitudes

LHA greater than 180° .... Zn = 180° - Z
LHA less than 180° .... Zn = 180° + Z

Form 104, All Sights, Pub. 249 or Pub. 229

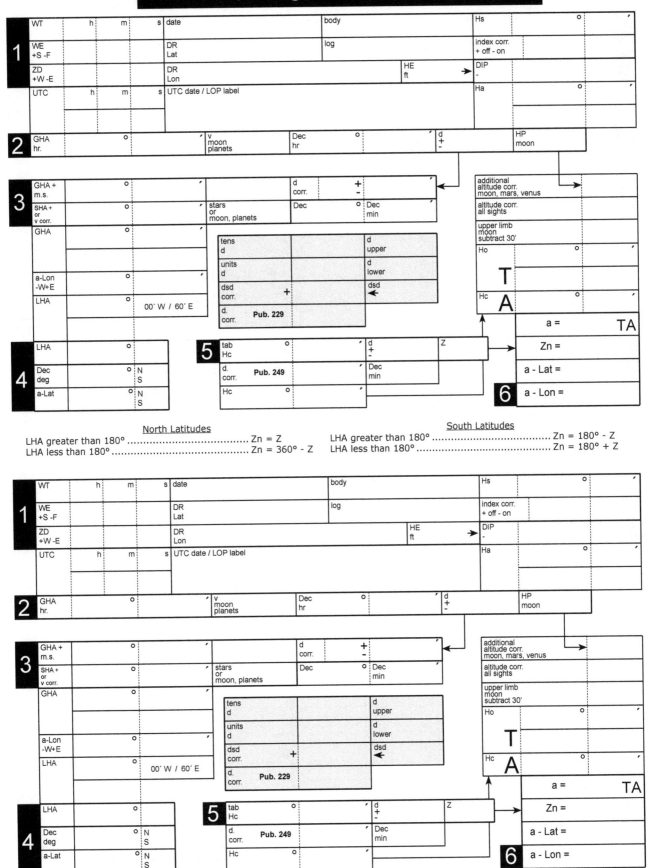

North Latitudes

LHA greater than 180° .... Zn = Z
LHA less than 180° .... Zn = 360° - Z

South Latitudes

LHA greater than 180° .... Zn = 180° - Z
LHA less than 180° .... Zn = 180° + Z

Form 104, All Sights, Pub. 249 or Pub. 229

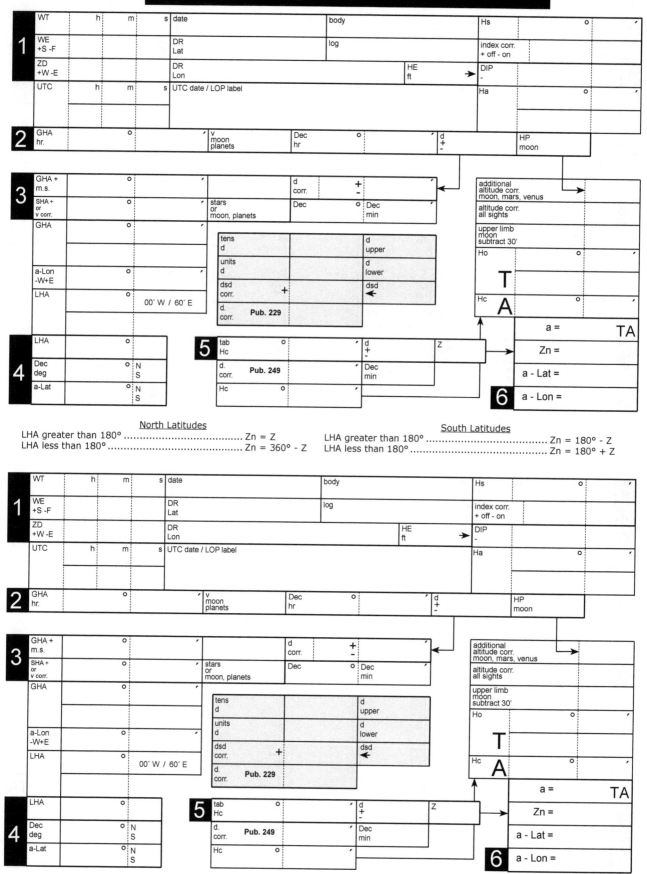

North Latitudes

LHA greater than 180° .... Zn = Z
LHA less than 180° .... Zn = 360° - Z

South Latitudes

LHA greater than 180° .... Zn = 180° - Z
LHA less than 180° .... Zn = 180° + Z

Form 104, All Sights, Pub. 249 or Pub. 229

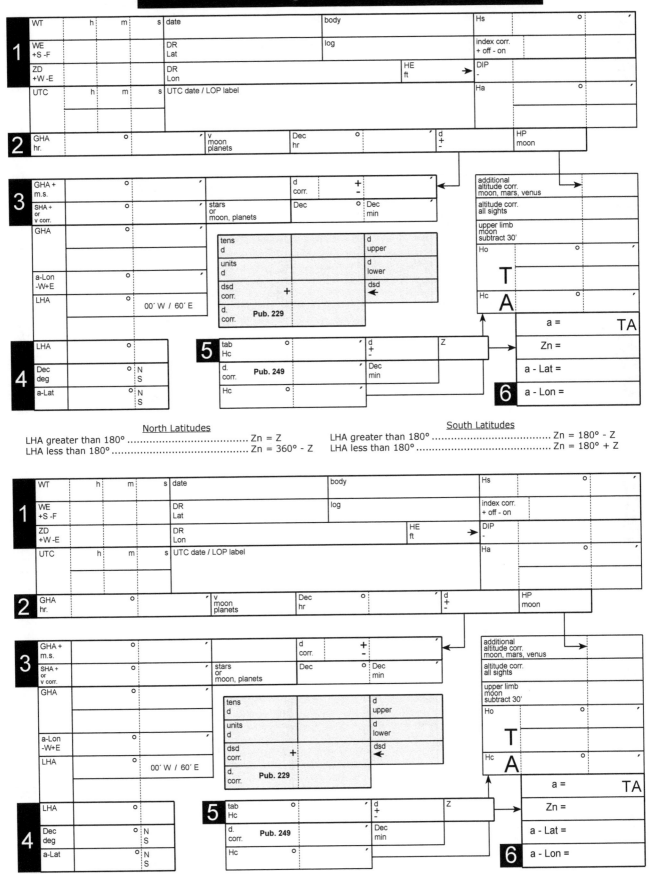

North Latitudes

LHA greater than 180° .... Zn = Z
LHA less than 180° .... Zn = 360° - Z

South Latitudes

LHA greater than 180° .... Zn = 180° - Z
LHA less than 180° .... Zn = 180° + Z

Form 104, All Sights, Pub. 249 or Pub. 229

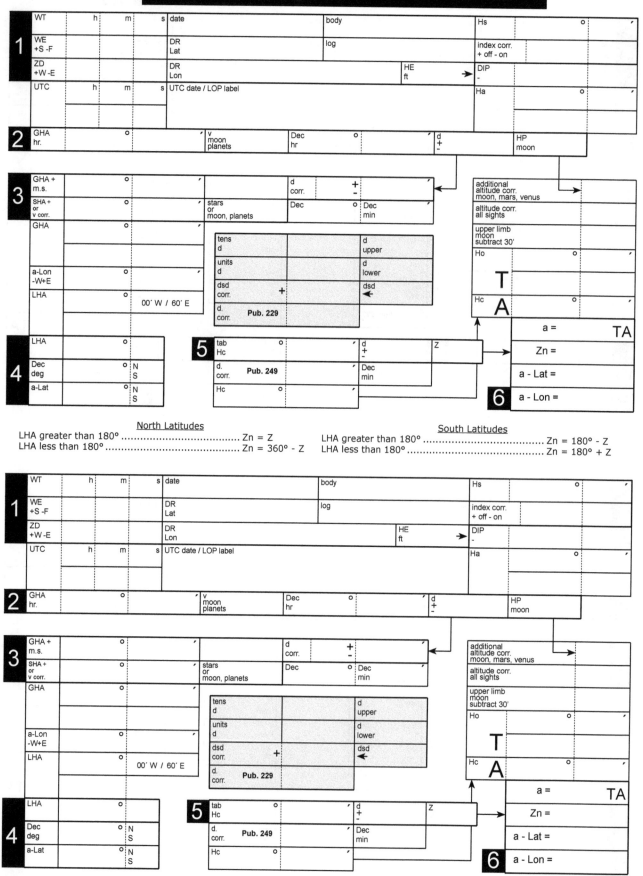

North Latitudes

LHA greater than 180° .... Zn = Z

LHA less than 180° .... Zn = 360° - Z

South Latitudes

LHA greater than 180° .... Zn = 180° - Z

LHA less than 180° .... Zn = 180° + Z

Form 104, All Sights, Pub. 249 or Pub. 229

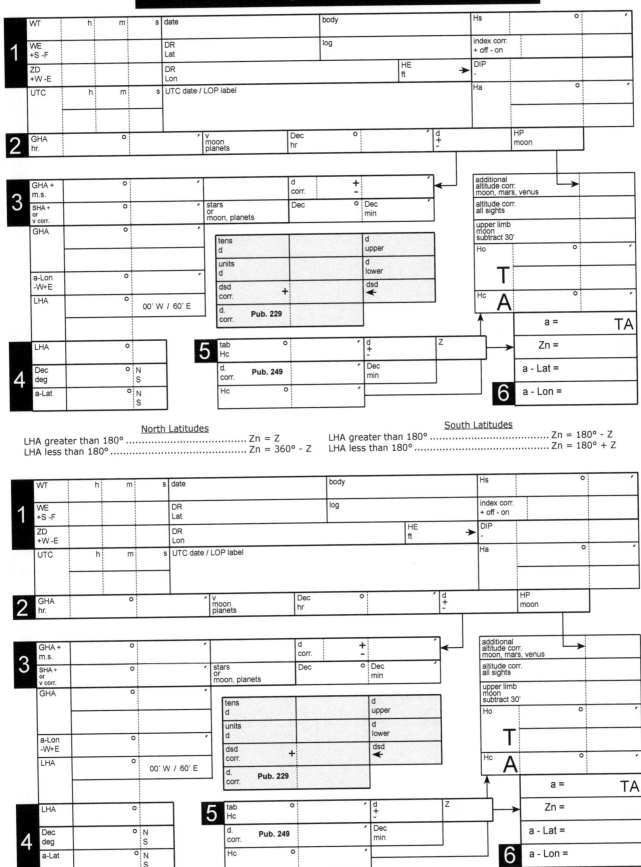

1	WT	h m s	date	body	Hs	°	'
	WE +S -F		DR Lat	log	index corr. + off - on		
	ZD +W -E		DR Lon	HE ft →	DIP -		
	UTC	h m s	UTC date / LOP label		Ha	°	'

| **2** | GHA hr. | ° | ' | v moon planets | Dec hr | ° | ' | d + - | HP moon |

3	GHA + m.s.	°	'		d corr.	+ -	'	additional altitude corr. moon, mars, venus
	SHA + or v corr.	°	'	stars or moon, planets	Dec	°	Dec min	altitude corr. all sights
	GHA	°	'					upper limb moon subtract 30'

tens d | | d upper
units d | | d lower
dsd corr. | + | dsd
d. corr. | **Pub. 229** |

| a-Lon -W+E | ° | ' |
| LHA | ° | 00' W / 60' E |

Ho | ° | '
Hc | ° | '

T A

a = TA

4	LHA	°
	Dec deg	° N S
	a-Lat	° N S

5	tab Hc	°	'	d + -	Z
	d. corr.	**Pub. 249**	'	Dec min
	Hc	°	'

Zn =
a - Lat =
6 a - Lon =

Underlined headings:

North Latitudes
LHA greater than 180° .... Zn = Z
LHA less than 180° .... Zn = 360° - Z

South Latitudes
LHA greater than 180° .... Zn = 180° - Z
LHA less than 180° .... Zn = 180° + Z

1	WT	h m s	date	body	Hs	°	'
	WE +S -F		DR Lat	log	index corr. + off - on		
	ZD +W -E		DR Lon	HE ft →	DIP -		
	UTC	h m s	UTC date / LOP label		Ha	°	'

| **2** | GHA hr. | ° | ' | v moon planets | Dec hr | ° | ' | d + - | HP moon |

3	GHA + m.s.	°	'		d corr.	+ -	'	additional altitude corr. moon, mars, venus
	SHA + or v corr.	°	'	stars or moon, planets	Dec	°	Dec min	altitude corr. all sights
	GHA	°	'					upper limb moon subtract 30'

tens d | | d upper
units d | | d lower
dsd corr. | + | dsd
d. corr. | **Pub. 229** |

| a-Lon -W+E | ° | ' |
| LHA | ° | 00' W / 60' E |

Ho | ° | '
Hc | ° | '

T A

a = TA

4	LHA	°
	Dec deg	° N S
	a-Lat	° N S

5	tab Hc	°	'	d + -	Z
	d. corr.	**Pub. 249**	'	Dec min
	Hc	°	'

Zn =
a - Lat =
6 a - Lon =

Form 104, All Sights, Pub. 249 or Pub. 229

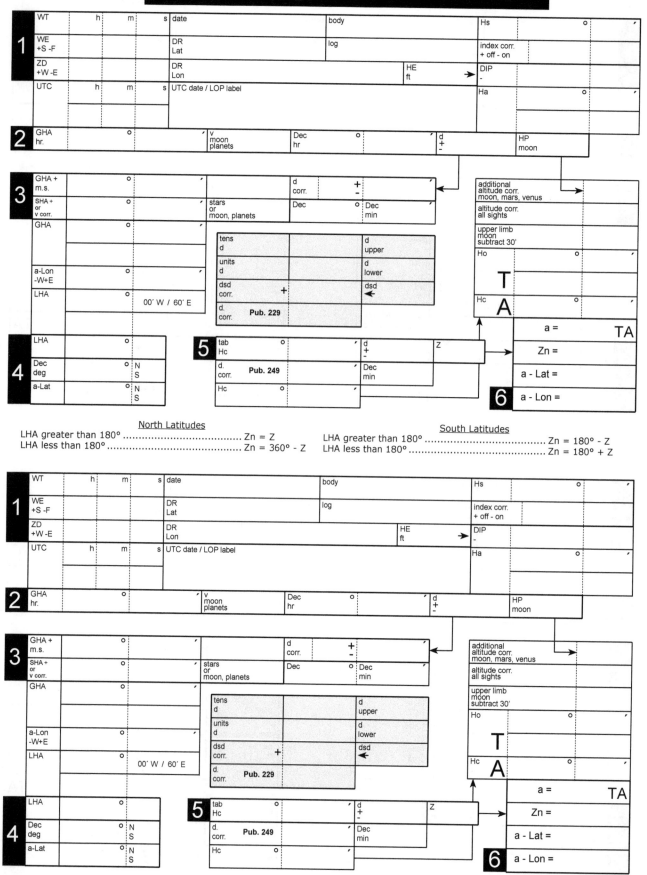

North Latitudes

LHA greater than 180° .... Zn = Z
LHA less than 180° .... Zn = 360° - Z

South Latitudes

LHA greater than 180° .... Zn = 180° - Z
LHA less than 180° .... Zn = 180° + Z

Form 104, All Sights, Pub. 249 or Pub. 229

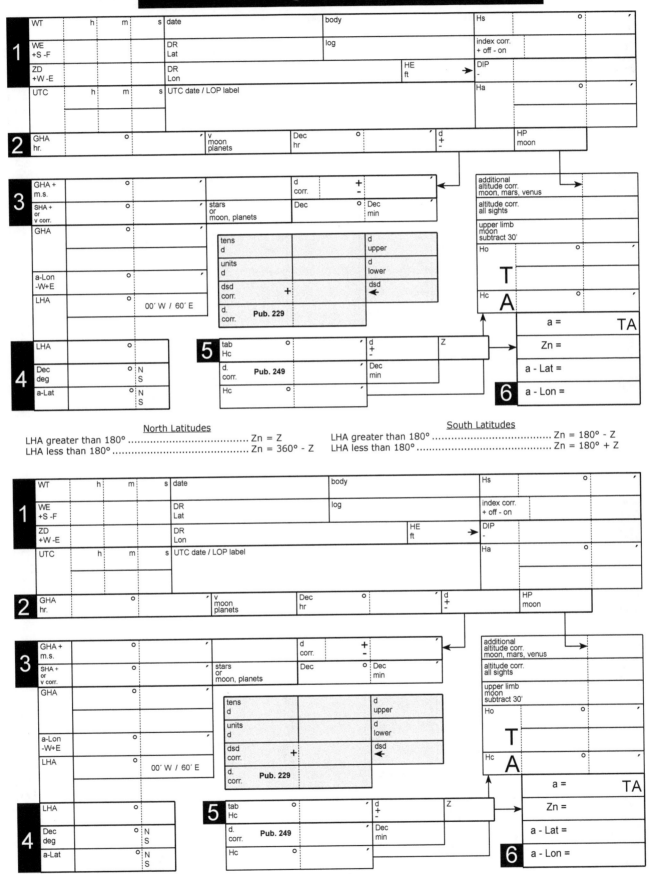

North Latitudes

LHA greater than 180° .... Zn = Z
LHA less than 180° .... Zn = 360° - Z

South Latitudes

LHA greater than 180° .... Zn = 180° - Z
LHA less than 180° .... Zn = 180° + Z

Form 104, All Sights, Pub. 249 or Pub. 229

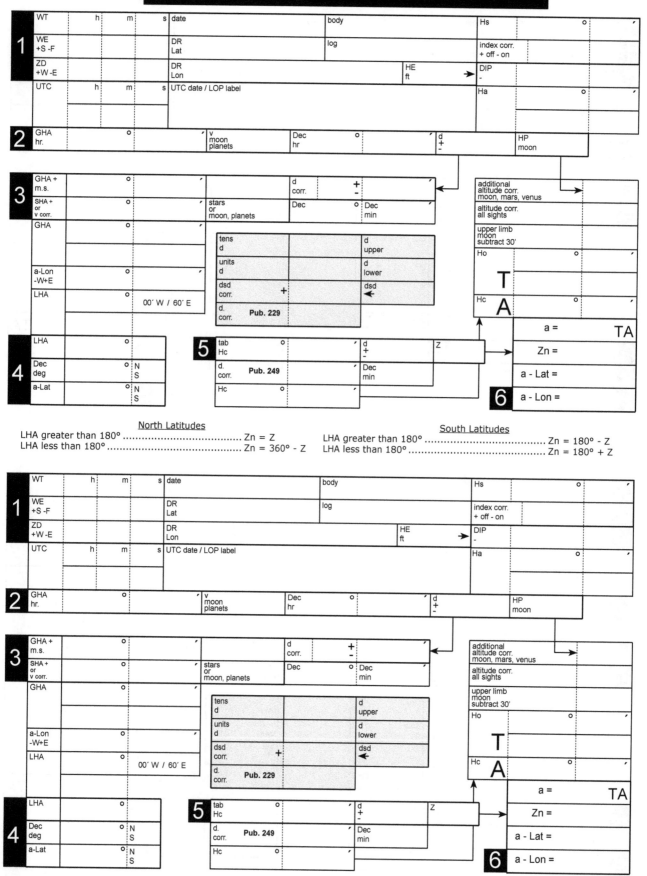

North Latitudes

LHA greater than 180° .... Zn = Z
LHA less than 180° .... Zn = 360° - Z

South Latitudes

LHA greater than 180° .... Zn = 180° - Z
LHA less than 180° .... Zn = 180° + Z

Form 104, All Sights, Pub. 249 or Pub. 229

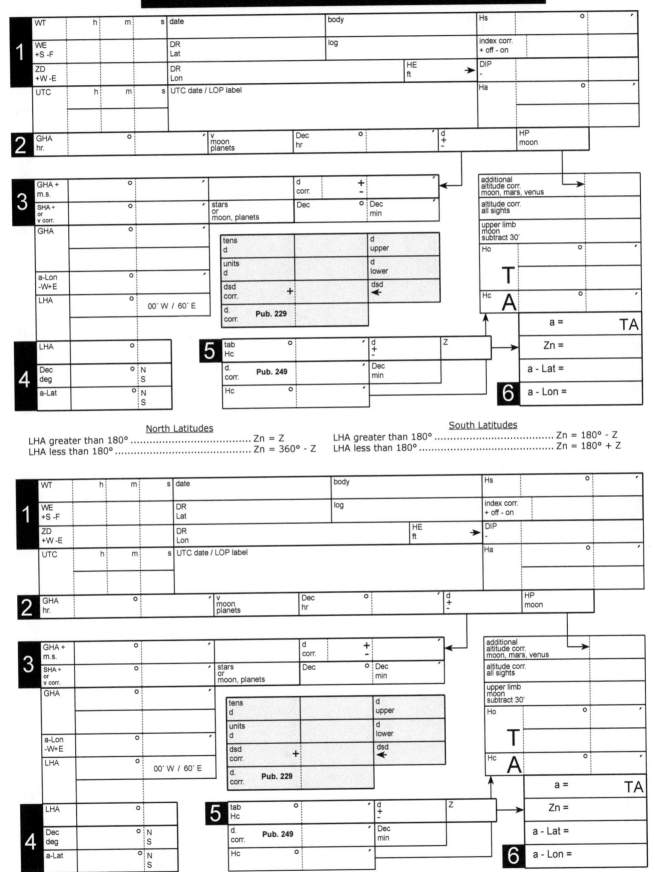

North Latitudes

LHA greater than 180° .... Zn = Z

LHA less than 180° .... Zn = 360° - Z

South Latitudes

LHA greater than 180° .... Zn = 180° - Z

LHA less than 180° .... Zn = 180° + Z

Form 104, All Sights, Pub. 249 or Pub. 229

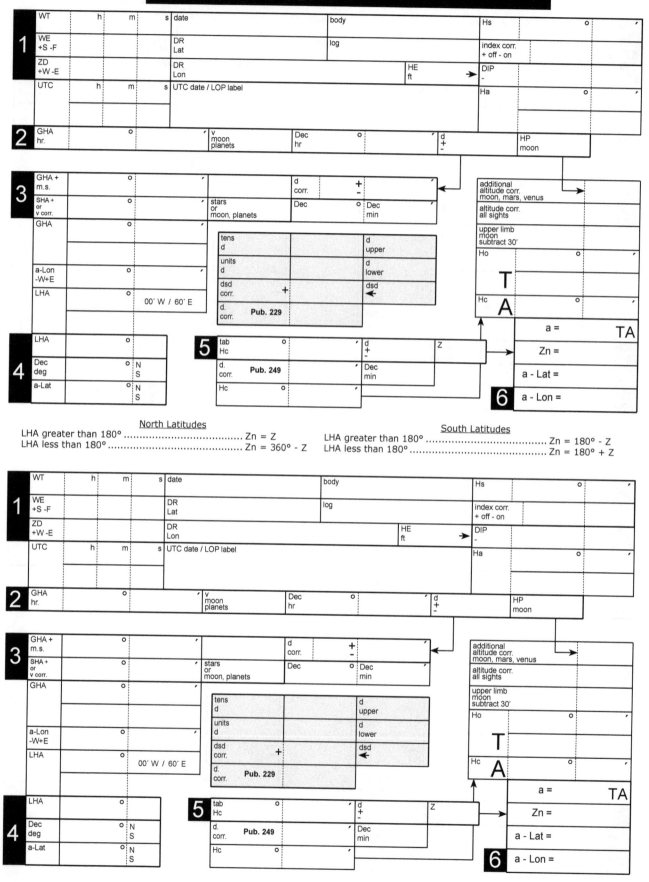

North Latitudes

LHA greater than 180° .... Zn = Z
LHA less than 180° .... Zn = 360° - Z

South Latitudes

LHA greater than 180° .... Zn = 180° - Z
LHA less than 180° .... Zn = 180° + Z

Form 104, All Sights, Pub. 249 or Pub. 229

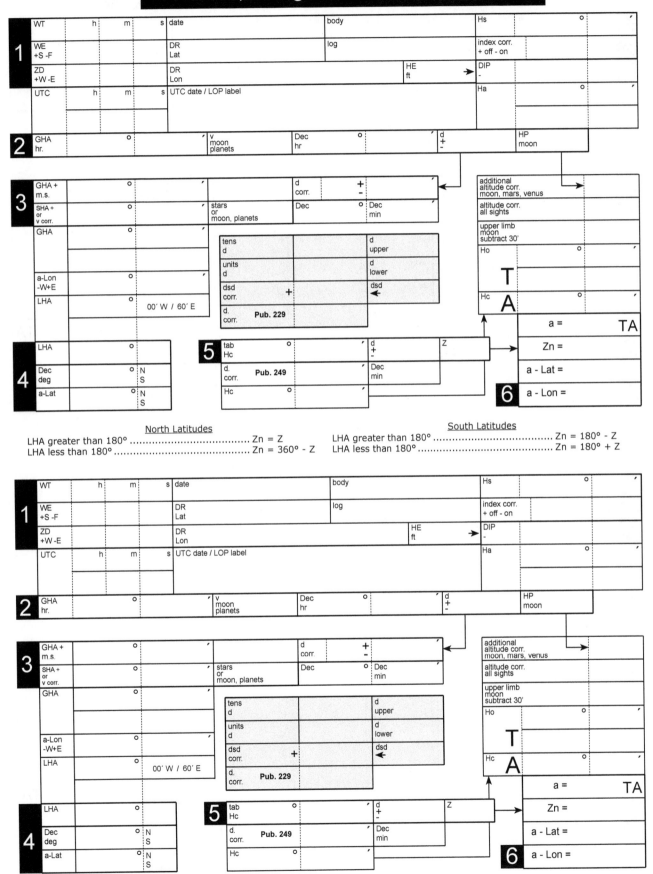

North Latitudes

LHA greater than 180° .... Zn = Z
LHA less than 180° .... Zn = 360° - Z

South Latitudes

LHA greater than 180° .... Zn = 180° - Z
LHA less than 180° .... Zn = 180° + Z

Form 104, All Sights, Pub. 249 or Pub. 229

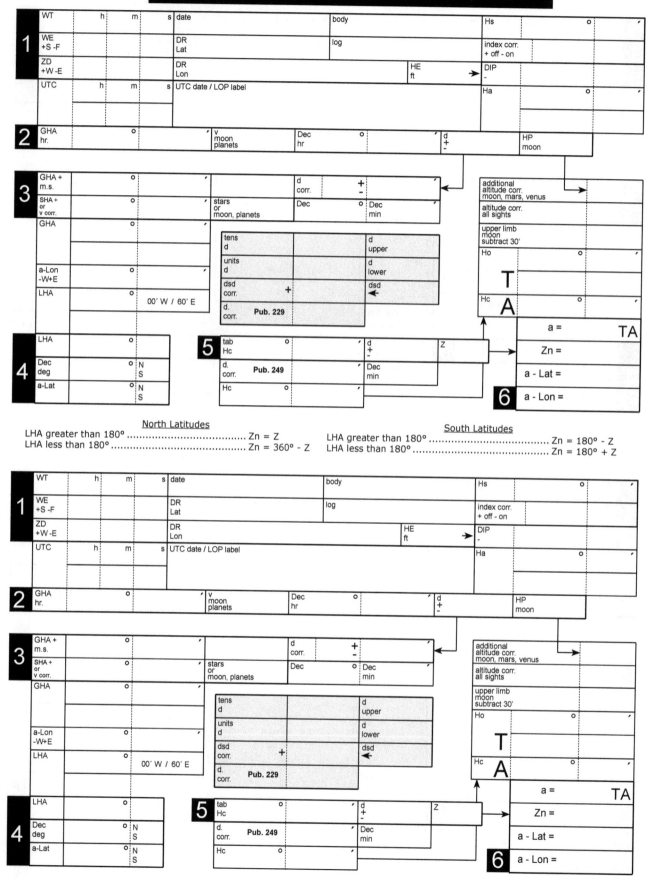

North Latitudes

LHA greater than 180° .... Zn = Z
LHA less than 180° .... Zn = 360° - Z

South Latitudes

LHA greater than 180° .... Zn = 180° - Z
LHA less than 180° .... Zn = 180° + Z

Form 104, All Sights, Pub. 249 or Pub. 229

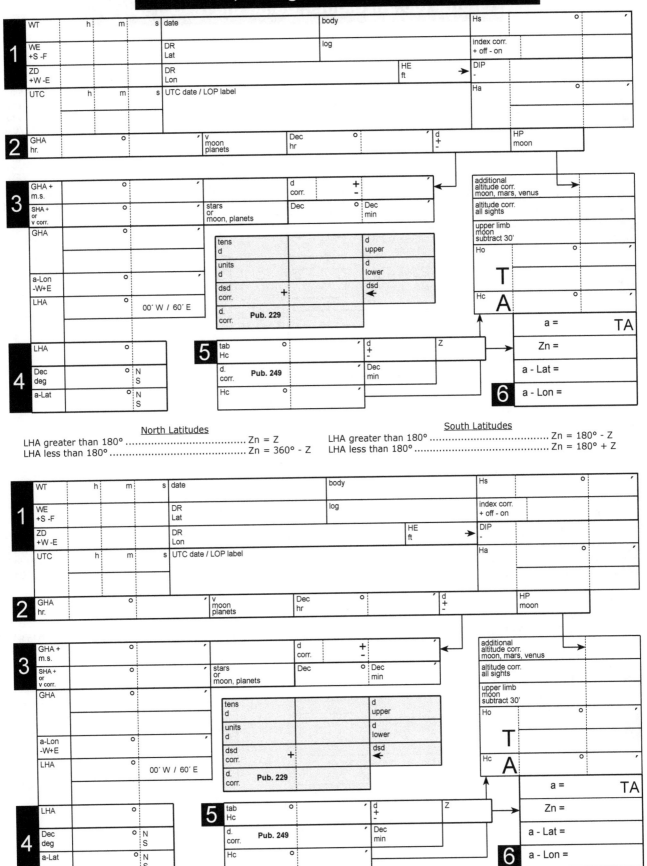

North Latitudes

LHA greater than 180° .... Zn = Z

LHA less than 180° .... Zn = 360° - Z

South Latitudes

LHA greater than 180° .... Zn = 180° - Z

LHA less than 180° .... Zn = 180° + Z

Form 106, All Sights, Using the NAO Tables

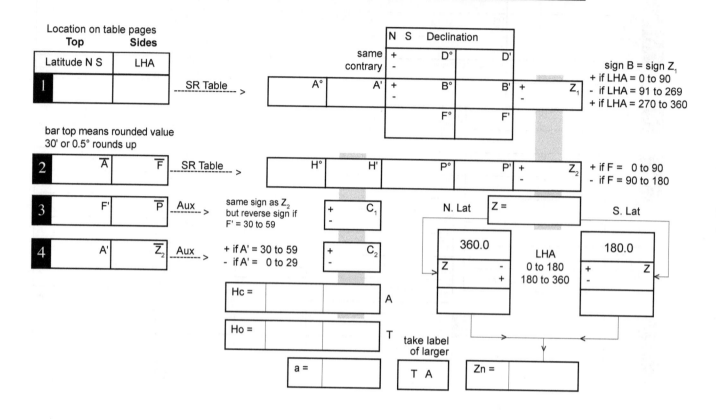

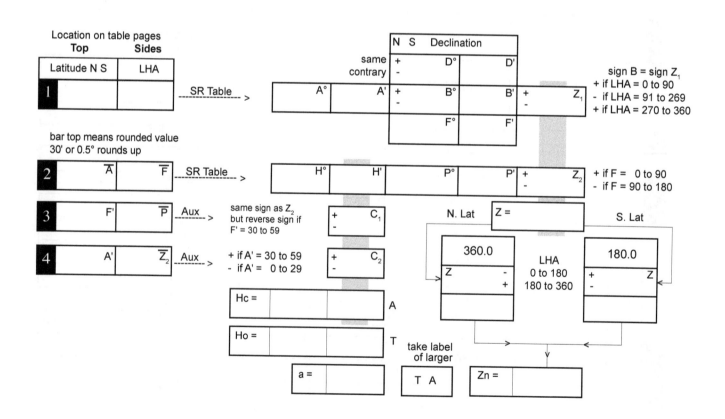

Form 106, All Sights, Using the NAO Tables

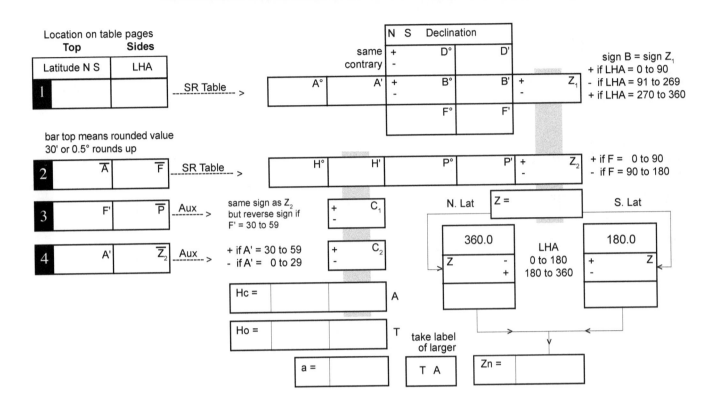

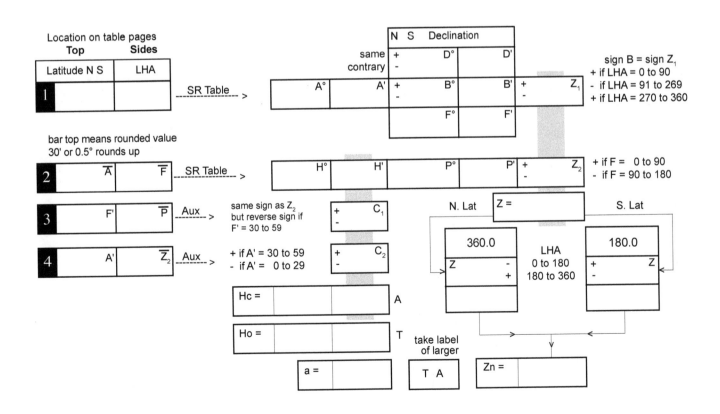

Form 106, All Sights, Using the NAO Tables

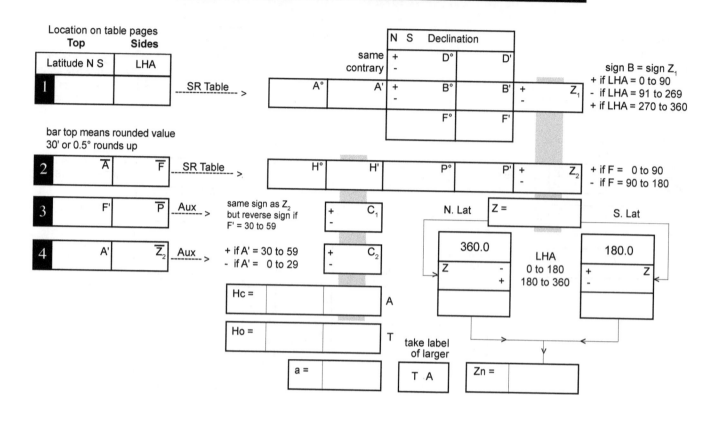

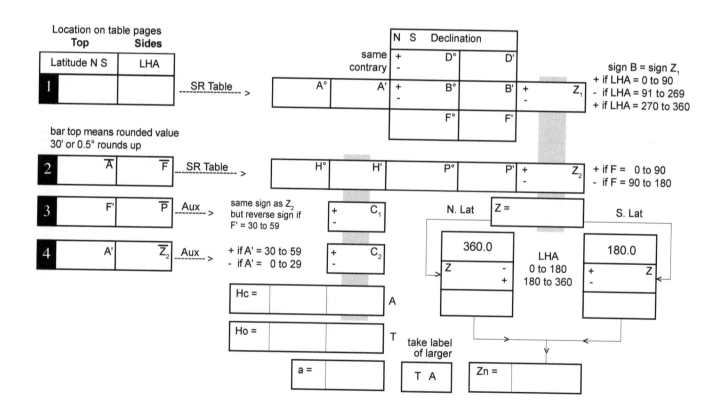

Form 106, All Sights, Using the NAO Tables

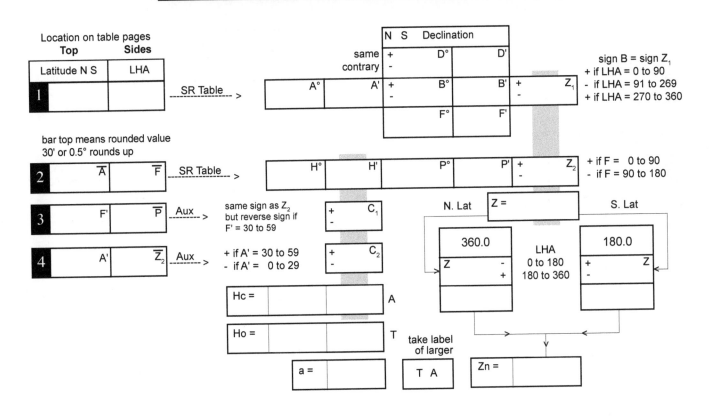

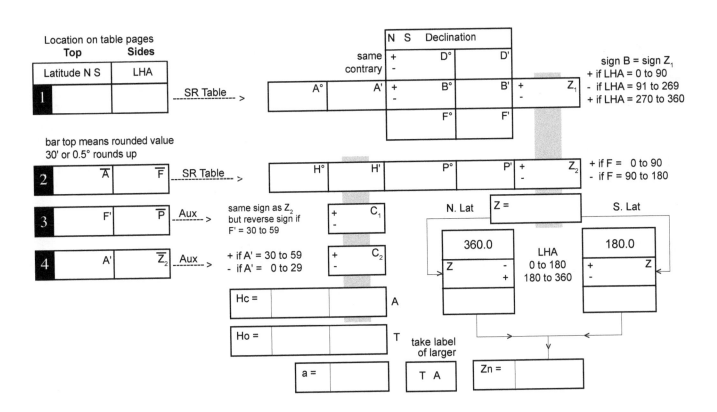

Form 106, All Sights, Using the NAO Tables

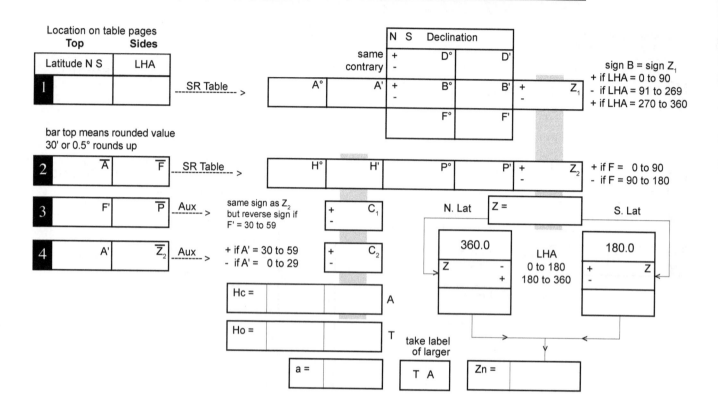

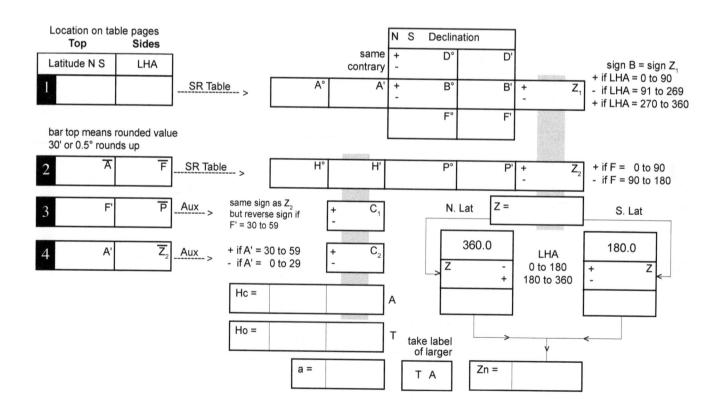

Form 106, All Sights, Using the NAO Tables

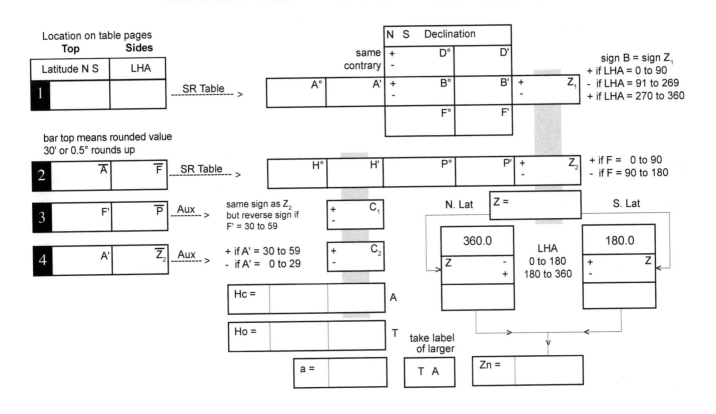

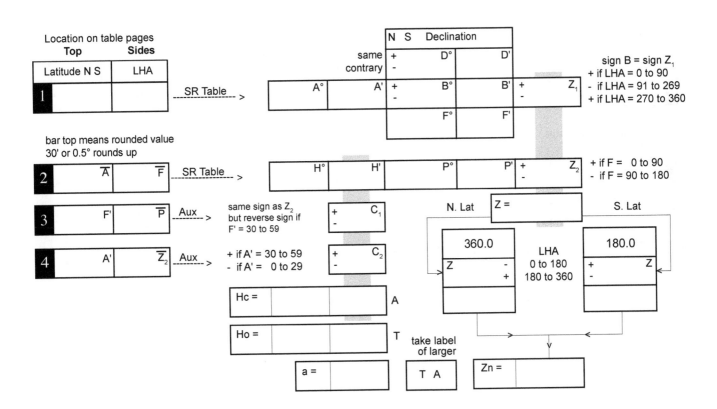

Form 106, All Sights, Using the NAO Tables

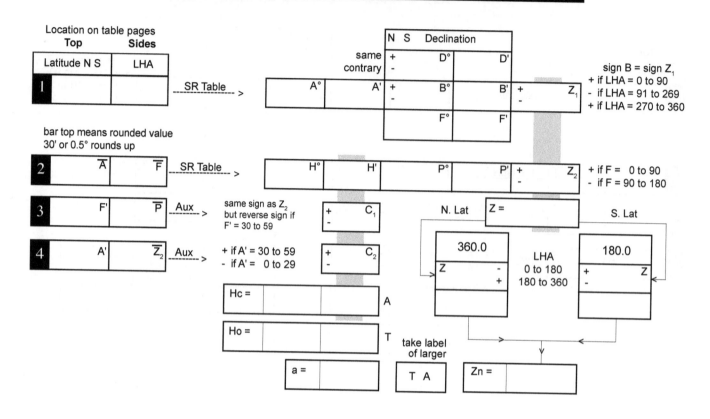

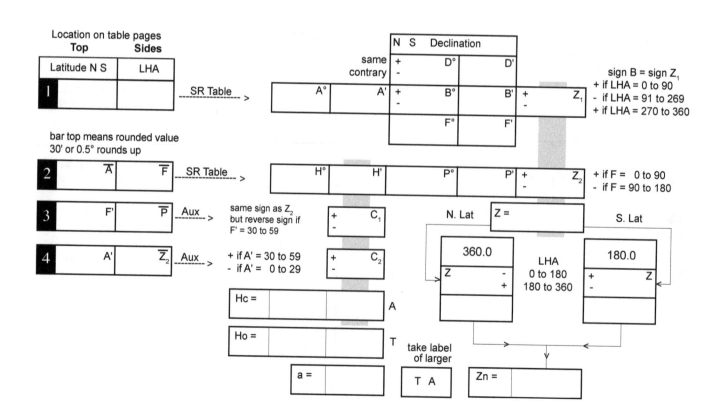

Form 106, All Sights, Using the NAO Tables

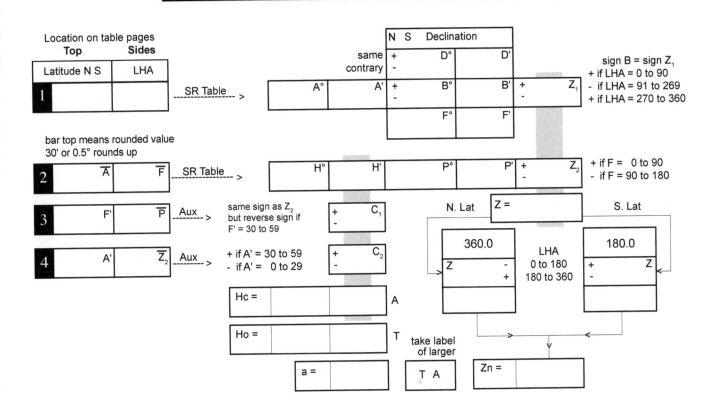

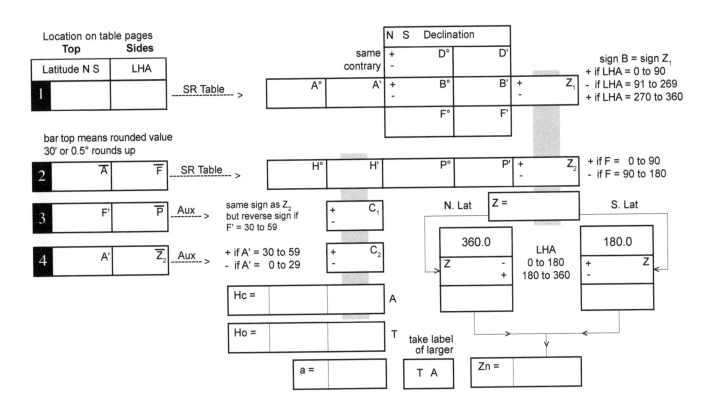

Form 106, All Sights, Using the NAO Tables

Form 106, All Sights, Using the NAO Tables

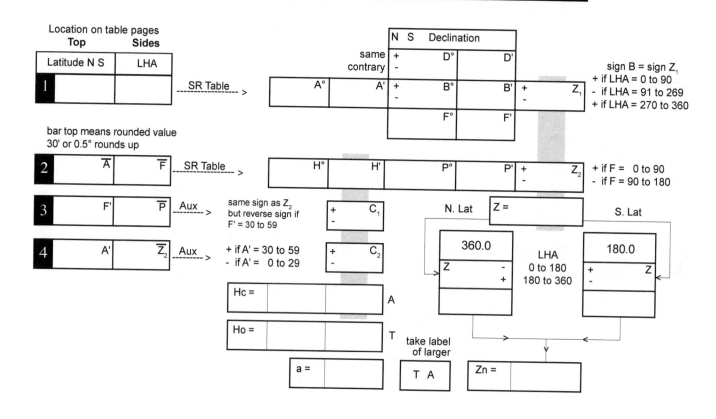

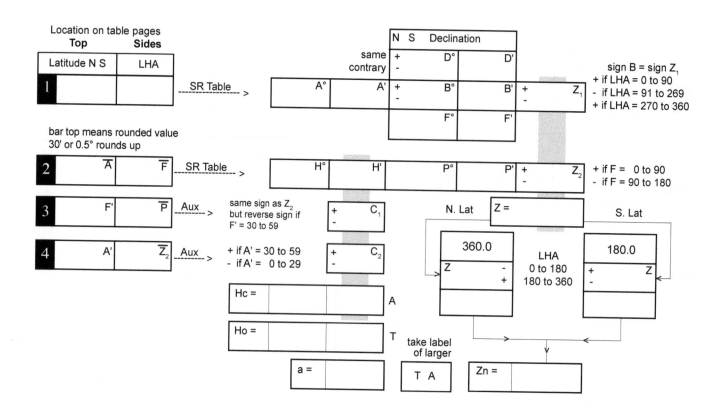

Form 106, All Sights, Using the NAO Tables

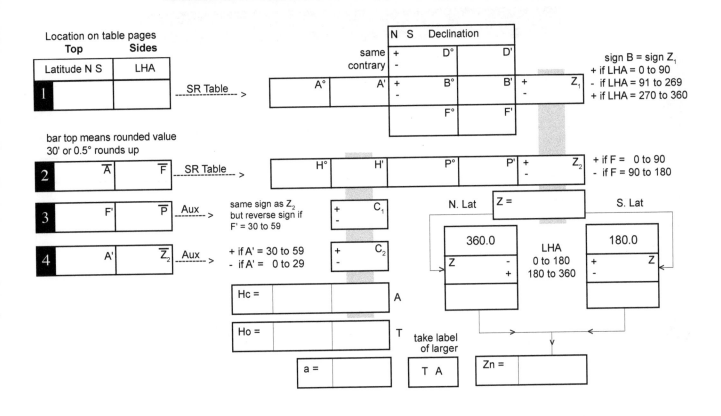

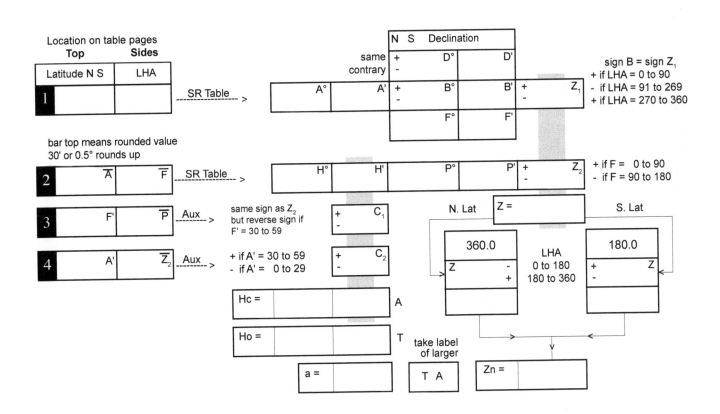

Form 108, All Bodies, Almanac, and NAO Tables

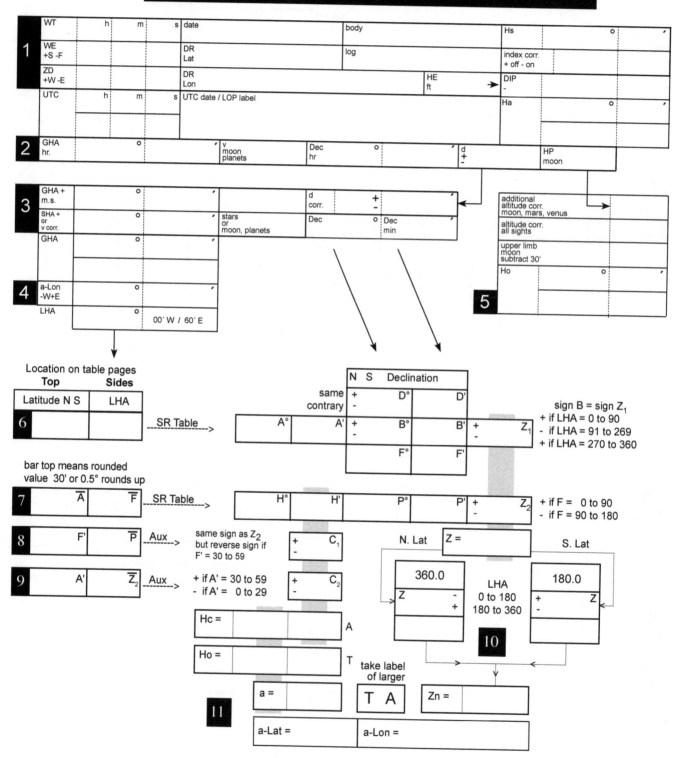

Form 108, All Bodies, Almanac, and NAO Tables

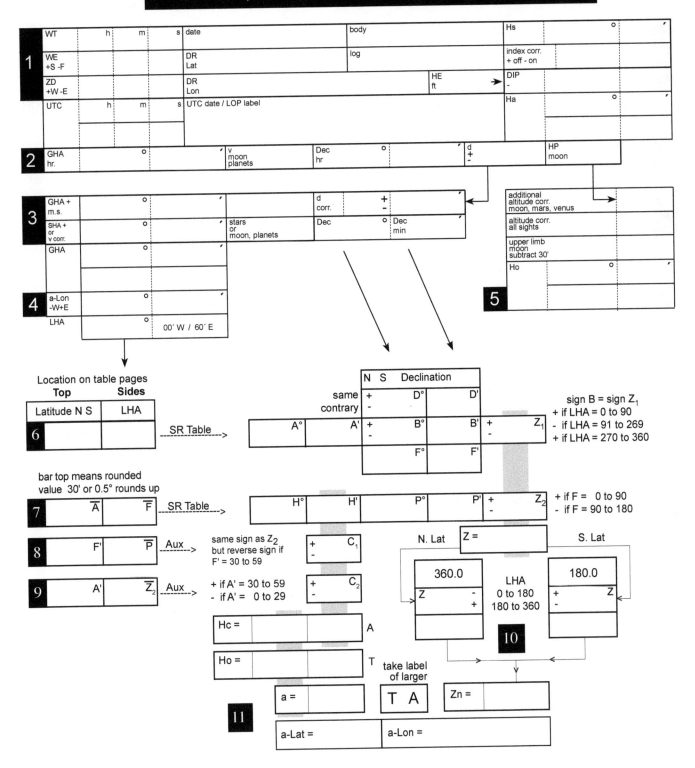

Form 108, All Bodies, Almanac, and NAO Tables

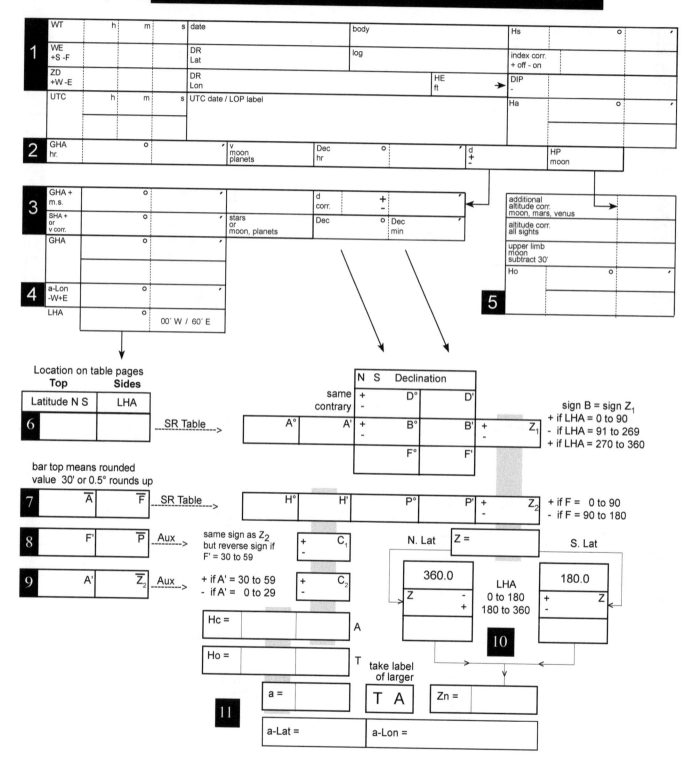

Form 108, All Bodies, Almanac, and NAO Tables

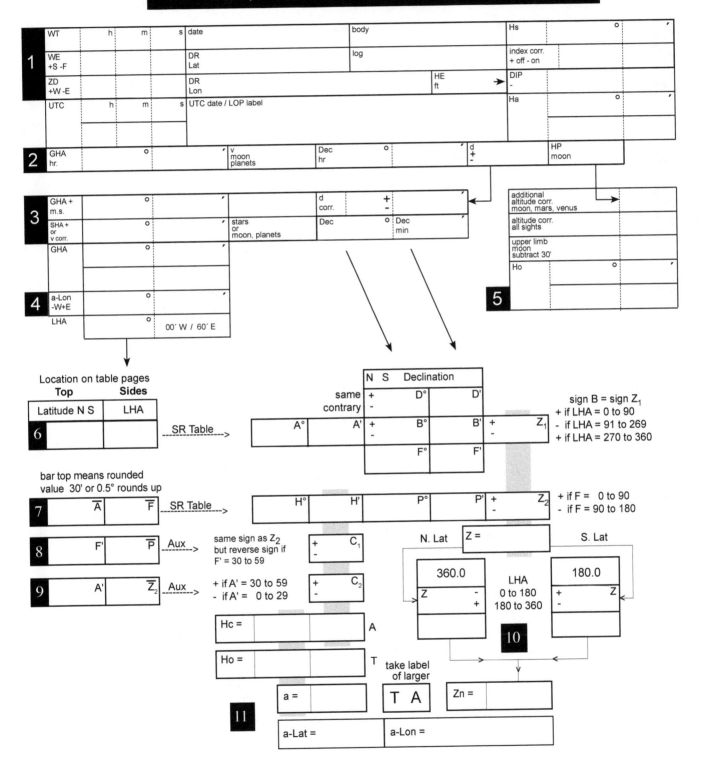

Form 108, All Bodies, Almanac, and NAO Tables

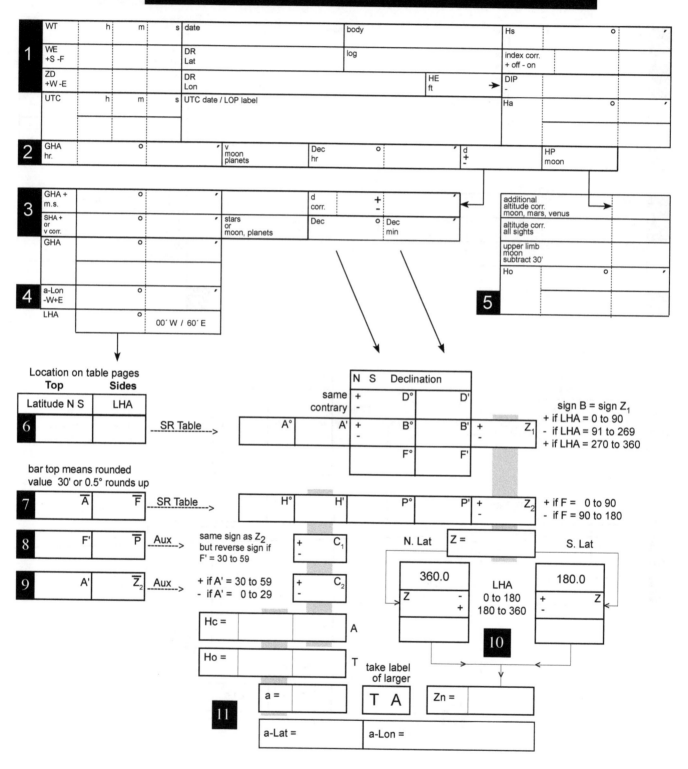

Form 108, All Bodies, Almanac, and NAO Tables

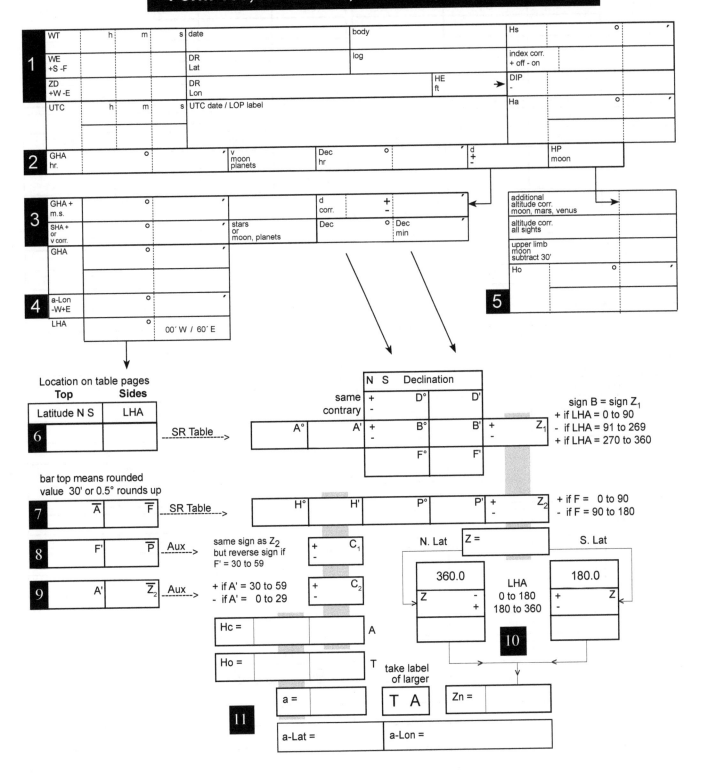

Form 109, for Solar Index Correction

Toward or Away		Date	
On	Off	Diff	Check SD
sight #	-	-	+
	=	= ÷2	= ÷4
SD=		=	=

Toward or Away		Date	
On	Off	Diff	Check SD
sight #	-	-	+
	=	= ÷2	= ÷4
SD=		=	=

Toward or Away		Date	
On	Off	Diff	Check SD
sight #	-	-	+
	=	= ÷2	= ÷4
SD=		=	=

Toward or Away		Date	
On	Off	Diff	Check SD
sight #	-	-	+
	=	= ÷2	= ÷4
SD=		=	=

Toward or Away		Date	
On	Off	Diff	Check SD
sight #	-	-	+
	=	= ÷2	= ÷4
SD=		=	=

Toward or Away		Date	
On	Off	Diff	Check SD
sight #	-	-	+
	=	= ÷2	= ÷4
SD=		=	=

Toward or Away		Date	
On	Off	Diff	Check SD
sight #	-	-	+
	=	= ÷2	= ÷4
SD=		=	=

Toward or Away		Date	
On	Off	Diff	Check SD
sight #	-	-	+
	=	= ÷2	= ÷4
SD=		=	=

Toward or Away		Date	
On	Off	Diff	Check SD
sight #	-	-	+
	=	= ÷2	= ÷4
SD=		=	=

Toward or Away		Date	
On	Off	Diff	Check SD
sight #	-	-	+
	=	= ÷2	= ÷4
SD=		=	=

Toward or Away		Date	
On	Off	Diff	Check SD
sight #	-	-	+
	=	= ÷2	= ÷4
SD=		=	=

Toward or Away		Date	
On	Off	Diff	Check SD
sight #	-	-	+
	=	= ÷2	= ÷4
SD=		=	=

This form covers 12 sights.

Form 109, for Solar Index Correction

Toward or Away		Date	
On	Off	Diff	Check SD
sight # -	-	+	
=	= ÷2	= ÷4	
SD=	=	=	

Toward or Away		Date	
On	Off	Diff	Check SD
sight # -	-	+	
=	= ÷2	= ÷4	
SD=	=	=	

Toward or Away		Date	
On	Off	Diff	Check SD
sight # -	-	+	
=	= ÷2	= ÷4	
SD=	=	=	

Toward or Away		Date	
On	Off	Diff	Check SD
sight # -	-	+	
=	= ÷2	= ÷4	
SD=	=	=	

Toward or Away		Date	
On	Off	Diff	Check SD
sight # -	-	+	
=	= ÷2	= ÷4	
SD=	=	=	

Toward or Away		Date	
On	Off	Diff	Check SD
sight # -	-	+	
=	= ÷2	= ÷4	
SD=	=	=	

Toward or Away		Date	
On	Off	Diff	Check SD
sight # -	-	+	
=	= ÷2	= ÷4	
SD=	=	=	

Toward or Away		Date	
On	Off	Diff	Check SD
sight # -	-	+	
=	= ÷2	= ÷4	
SD=	=	=	

Toward or Away		Date	
On	Off	Diff	Check SD
sight # -	-	+	
=	= ÷2	= ÷4	
SD=	=	=	

Toward or Away		Date	
On	Off	Diff	Check SD
sight # -	-	+	
=	= ÷2	= ÷4	
SD=	=	=	

Toward or Away		Date	
On	Off	Diff	Check SD
sight # -	-	+	
=	= ÷2	= ÷4	
SD=	=	=	

Toward or Away		Date	
On	Off	Diff	Check SD
sight # -	-	+	
=	= ÷2	= ÷4	
SD=	=	=	

This form covers 12 sights.

Form 109, for Solar Index Correction

Toward or Away		Date	
On	Off	Diff	Check SD
sight #	-	-	+
	=	= ÷2	= ÷4
SD=	=	=

Toward or Away		Date	
On	Off	Diff	Check SD
sight #	-	-	+
	=	= ÷2	= ÷4
SD=	=	=

Toward or Away		Date	
On	Off	Diff	Check SD
sight #	-	-	+
	=	= ÷2	= ÷4
SD=	=	=

Toward or Away		Date	
On	Off	Diff	Check SD
sight #	-	-	+
	=	= ÷2	= ÷4
SD=	=	=

Toward or Away		Date	
On	Off	Diff	Check SD
sight #	-	-	+
	=	= ÷2	= ÷4
SD=	=	=

Toward or Away		Date	
On	Off	Diff	Check SD
sight #	-	-	+
	=	= ÷2	= ÷4
SD=	=	=

Toward or Away		Date	
On	Off	Diff	Check SD
sight #	-	-	+
	=	= ÷2	= ÷4
SD=	=	=

Toward or Away		Date	
On	Off	Diff	Check SD
sight #	-	-	+
	=	= ÷2	= ÷4
SD=	=	=

Toward or Away		Date	
On	Off	Diff	Check SD
sight #	-	-	+
	=	= ÷2	= ÷4
SD=	=	=

Toward or Away		Date	
On	Off	Diff	Check SD
sight #	-	-	+
	=	= ÷2	= ÷4
SD=	=	=

Toward or Away		Date	
On	Off	Diff	Check SD
sight #	-	-	+
	=	= ÷2	= ÷4
SD=	=	=

Toward or Away		Date	
On	Off	Diff	Check SD
sight #	-	-	+
	=	= ÷2	= ÷4
SD=	=	=

This form covers 12 sights.

Form 109, for Solar Index Correction

Toward or Away		Date	
On	Off	Diff	Check SD
sight #	-	-	+
	=	= ÷2	= ÷4
SD=		=	=

Toward or Away		Date	
On	Off	Diff	Check SD
sight #	-	-	+
	=	= ÷2	= ÷4
SD=		=	=

Toward or Away		Date	
On	Off	Diff	Check SD
sight #	-	-	+
	=	= ÷2	= ÷4
SD=		=	=

Toward or Away		Date	
On	Off	Diff	Check SD
sight #	-	-	+
	=	= ÷2	= ÷4
SD=		=	=

Toward or Away		Date	
On	Off	Diff	Check SD
sight #	-	-	+
	=	= ÷2	= ÷4
SD=		=	=

Toward or Away		Date	
On	Off	Diff	Check SD
sight #	-	-	+
	=	= ÷2	= ÷4
SD=		=	=

Toward or Away		Date	
On	Off	Diff	Check SD
sight #	-	-	+
	=	= ÷2	= ÷4
SD=		=	=

Toward or Away		Date	
On	Off	Diff	Check SD
sight #	-	-	+
	=	= ÷2	= ÷4
SD=		=	=

Toward or Away		Date	
On	Off	Diff	Check SD
sight #	-	-	+
	=	= ÷2	= ÷4
SD=		=	=

Toward or Away		Date	
On	Off	Diff	Check SD
sight #	-	-	+
	=	= ÷2	= ÷4
SD=		=	=

Toward or Away		Date	
On	Off	Diff	Check SD
sight #	-	-	+
	=	= ÷2	= ÷4
SD=		=	=

Toward or Away		Date	
On	Off	Diff	Check SD
sight #	-	-	+
	=	= ÷2	= ÷4
SD=		=	=

This form covers 12 sights.

Form 107, for Latitude at LAN

Step 1 Correct Hs to get Ho

				°		'
1-1	Record Maximum Sextant Height (Hs = peak height of the sun at noon), and mark limb	Lower Upper	Hs			
1-2	Record Index Correction (mark sign + if off, - if on)		IC	Off + On −		'
1-3	Record eye height (HE) and Look up Dip Correction on the right-hand side of Table A2, front of the Almanac (correction depends on HE)	Dip HE (ft)		−		'
1-4	Sum the above three numbers to get Apparent Height		Ha	°		'
1-5	Look up altitude correction on lefthand side of Table A2, front of the Almanac (correction depends on Ha, Limb, and month) (mark sign + for lower limb, - for upper limb)		Alt corr.	+ −		'
1-6	Sum the above two numbers to get Observed Height		Ho	°		'

Step 2 Determine the Zenith Distance   89° 60.0'

				°		'
2-1	Record Ho from Step 1, above, and then subtract it from 90° to get the zenith distance		Ho	−		
2-2	Zenith distance		z	°		'

Step 3 Use the Almanac to Find Sun's Declination   GMT date =

					°		'
3-1	Record the date and GMT of the sight (the time the sun reached its peak height)	GMT (hr) =		GMT (min) =			
3-2	Turn to the daily page of the Almanac for the date of the sight, and find the sun's declination (dec) for the hour of the sight (line 3-1) and record it here.	Dec (hr)		N S	°		'
3-3	Record the d-value from the bottom of the dec column in the Almanac. Mark the signs of the d-value and d-corr + if the dec for the next hour is larger, or - if it is smaller.	d-value =	+ −	d-corr =	+ −		'
3-4	Turn to the Increments and Corrections pages at the back of the Almanac (T-9 to 12, in the notes) and find the minutes table for the GMT minutes (line 3-1). On the right-hand side of the double line in the table, find the d-corr corresponding to the d-value of line 3-3.	Declination =		N S	°		'
		3-5 Apply the d-corr to the dec(hr) and record it above.					

Step 4 Find Latitude from Zenith Distance and Declination

Record DR Latitude to use as a guide, and then take the sum or difference of zenith distance and declination to find your true Latitude at LAN.

	°		'
Declination or Zenith distance			
Zenith distance or Declination	°		'
Latitude =	°		'

Form 107, for Latitude at LAN

Step 1 Correct Hs to get Ho

				°	'
1-1	Record Maximum Sextant Height (Hs = peak height of the sun at noon), and mark limb	Lower Upper	Hs		
1-2	Record Index Correction (mark sign + if off, - if on)	IC	Off + On −		'
1-3	Record eye height (HE) and Look up Dip Correction on the right-hand side of Table A2, front of the Almanac (correction depends on HE)	Dip HE (ft)	−		'
1-4	Sum the above three numbers to get Apparent Height	Ha		°	'
1-5	Look up altitude correction on lefthand side of Table A2, front of the Almanac (correction depends on Ha, Limb, and month) (mark sign + for lower limb, - for upper limb)	Alt corr.	+ −		'
1-6	Sum the above two numbers to get Observed Height	Ho		°	'

Step 2 Determine the Zenith Distance — 89° 60.0'

				°	'
2-1	Record Ho from Step 1, above, and then subtract it from 90° to get the zenith distance	Ho	−		
2-2	Zenith distance	z		°	'

Step 3 Use the Almanac to Find Sun's Declination — GMT date =

				°	'
3-1	Record the date and GMT of the sight (the time the sun reached its peak height)	GMT (hr) =	GMT (min) =		
3-2	Turn to the daily page of the Almanac for the date of the sight, and find the sun's declination (dec) for the hour of the sight (line 3-1) and record it here.	Dec (hr)	N S	°	'
3-3	Record the d-value from the bottom of the dec column in the Almanac. Mark the signs of the d-value and d-corr + if the dec for the next hour is larger, or - if it is smaller.	d-value = + −	d-corr = + −		'
3-4	Turn to the Increments and Corrections pages at the back of the Almanac (T-9 to 12, in the notes) and find the minutes table for the GMT minutes (line 3-1). On the right-hand side of the double line in the table, find the d-corr corresponding to the d-value of line 3-3.	Declination =	N S	°	'
		3-5 Apply the d-corr to the dec(hr) and record it above.			

Step 4 Find Latitude from Zenith Distance and Declination

Record DR Latitude to use as a guide, and then take the sum or difference of zenith distance and declination to find your true Latitude at LAN.

		°	'
Declination or Zenith distance			
Zenith distance or Declination		°	'
Latitude =		°	'

Form 107, for Latitude at LAN

Step 1 Correct Hs to get Ho

1-1	Record Maximum Sextant Height (Hs = peak height of the sun at noon), and mark limb	Lower Hs Upper	°	'
1-2	Record Index Correction (mark sign + if off, - if on)	IC	Off + On −	'
1-3	Record eye height (HE) and Look up Dip Correction on the right-hand side of Table A2, front of the Almanac (correction depends on HE)	Dip HE (ft)	−	'
1-4	Sum the above three numbers to get Apparent Height	Ha	°	'
1-5	Look up altitude correction on lefthand side of Table A2, front of the Almanac (correction depends on Ha, Limb, and month) (mark sign + for lower limb, - for upper limb)	Alt corr.	+ −	'
1-6	Sum the above two numbers to get Observed Height	Ho	°	'

Step 2 Determine the Zenith Distance   89° 60.0'

2-1	Record Ho from Step 1, above, and then subtract it from 90° to get the zenith distance	Ho	− °	'
2-2	Zenith distance	z	°	'

Step 3 Use the Almanac to Find Sun's Declination   GMT date =

3-1	Record the date and GMT of the sight (the time the sun reached its peak height)	GMT (hr) =	GMT (min) =	
3-2	Turn to the daily page of the Almanac for the date of the sight, and find the sun's declination (dec) for the hour of the sight (line 3-1) and record it here.	Dec (hr)	N S	° '
3-3	Record the d-value from the bottom of the dec column in the Almanac. Mark the signs of the d-value and d-corr + if the dec for the next hour is larger, or - if it is smaller.	d-value = + −	d-corr = + −	'
3-4	Turn to the Increments and Corrections pages at the back of the Almanac (T-9 to 12, in the notes) and find the minutes table for the GMT minutes (line 3-1). On the right-hand side of the double line in the table, find the d-corr corresponding to the d-value of line 3-3.	Declination =	N S	° '
		3-5 Apply the d-corr to the dec(hr) and record it above.		

Step 4 Find Latitude from Zenith Distance and Declination

Record DR Latitude to use as a guide, and then take the sum or difference of zenith distance and declination to find your true Latitude at LAN.

Declination or Zenith distance	°	'
Zenith distance or Declination	°	'
Latitude =	°	'

Form 107, for Latitude at LAN

Step 1   Correct Hs to get Ho

					°		'
1-1	Record Maximum Sextant Height (Hs = peak height of the sun at noon), and mark limb	Lower Upper	Hs				
1-2	Record Index Correction (mark sign + if off, - if on)	IC	Off On	+ −			'
1-3	Record eye height (HE) and Look up Dip Correction on the right-hand side of Table A2, front of the Almanac (correction depends on HE)	Dip HE (ft)		−			'
1-4	Sum the above three numbers to get Apparent Height	Ha			°		'
1-5	Look up altitude correction on lefthand side of Table A2, front of the Almanac (correction depends on Ha, Limb, and month) (mark sign + for lower limb, - for upper limb)	Alt corr.		+ −			'
1-6	Sum the above two numbers to get Observed Height	Ho			°		'

Step 2   Determine the Zenith Distance   89° 60.0'

				°		'
2-1	Record Ho from Step 1, above, and then subtract it from 90° to get the zenith distance	Ho	−			
2-2	Zenith distance	z			°	'

Step 3 Use the Almanac to Find Sun's Declination   GMT date =

					°	'
3-1	Record the date and GMT of the sight (the time the sun reached its peak height)	GMT (hr) =	GMT (min) =			
3-2	Turn to the daily page of the Almanac for the date of the sight, and find the sun's declination (dec) for the hour of the sight (line 3-1) and record it here.	Dec (hr)	N S			
3-3	Record the d-value from the bottom of the dec column in the Almanac. Mark the signs of the d-value and d-corr + if the dec for the next hour is larger, or - if it is smaller.	d-value = + −	d-corr = + −			'
3-4	Turn to the Increments and Corrections pages at the back of the Almanac (T-9 to 12, in the notes) and find the minutes table for the GMT minutes (line 3-1). On the right-hand side of the double line in the table, find the d-corr corresponding to the d-value of line 3-3.	Declination =	N S		°	'
		3-5 Apply the d-corr to the dec(hr) and record it above.				

Step 4 Find Latitude from Zenith Distance and Declination

Record DR Latitude to use as a guide, and then take the sum or difference of zenith distance and declination to find your true Latitude at LAN.

	°	'
Declination or Zenith distance		
Zenith distance or Declination	°	'
Latitude =	°	'

Form 107, for Latitude at LAN

Step 1   Correct Hs to get Ho

					°		'
1-1	Record Maximum Sextant Height (Hs = peak height of the sun at noon), and mark limb	Lower / Upper	Hs				
1-2	Record Index Correction (mark sign + if off, - if on)		IC	Off / On	+ / −		'
1-3	Record eye height (HE) and Look up Dip Correction on the right-hand side of Table A2, front of the Almanac (correction depends on HE)	Dip			−		'
		HE (ft)					
1-4	Sum the above three numbers to get Apparent Height		Ha		°		'
1-5	Look up altitude correction on lefthand side of Table A2, front of the Almanac (correction depends on Ha, Limb, and month) (mark sign + for lower limb, - for upper limb)		Alt corr.		+ / −		'
1-6	Sum the above two numbers to get Observed Height		Ho		°		'

Step 2   Determine the Zenith Distance   89° 60.0'

					°		'
2-1	Record Ho from Step 1, above, and then subtract it from 90° to get the zenith distance		Ho	−	°		'
2-2	Zenith distance		z		°		'

Step 3 Use the Almanac to Find Sun's Declination   GMT date =

					°		'
3-1	Record the date and GMT of the sight (the time the sun reached its peak height)	GMT (hr) =		GMT (min) =			
3-2	Turn to the daily page of the Almanac for the date of the sight, and find the sun's declination (dec) for the hour of the sight (line 3-1) and record it here.	Dec (hr)		N / S		°		'
3-3	Record the d-value from the bottom of the dec column in the Almanac. Mark the signs of the d-value and d-corr + if the dec for the next hour is larger, or - if it is smaller.	d-value =	+ / −	d-corr =	+ / −		'
3-4	Turn to the Increments and Corrections pages at the back of the Almanac (T-9 to 12, in the notes) and find the minutes table for the GMT minutes (line 3-1). On the right-hand side of the double line in the table, find the d-corr corresponding to the d-value of line 3-3.	Declination =		N / S		°		'
		3-5 Apply the d-corr to the dec(hr) and record it above.						

Step 4 Find Latitude from Zenith Distance and Declination

Record DR Latitude to use as a guide, and then take the sum or difference of zenith distance and declination to find your true Latitude at LAN.

	°		'
Declination or Zenith distance			
Zenith distance or Declination			
Latitude =			

Form 107, for Latitude at LAN

Step 1   Correct Hs to get Ho

					°	'
1-1	Record Maximum Sextant Height (Hs = peak height of the sun at noon), and mark limb	Lower Upper	Hs			
1-2	Record Index Correction (mark sign + if off, - if on)		IC	Off + On −		'
1-3	Record eye height (HE) and Look up Dip Correction on the right-hand side of Table A2, front of the Almanac (correction depends on HE)	Dip HE (ft)		−		'
1-4	Sum the above three numbers to get Apparent Height		Ha		°	'
1-5	Look up altitude correction on lefthand side of Table A2, front of the Almanac (correction depends on Ha, Limb, and month) (mark sign + for lower limb, - for upper limb)		Alt corr.	+ −		'
1-6	Sum the above two numbers to get Observed Height		Ho		°	'

Step 2   Determine the Zenith Distance   89°   60.0'

				°	'
2-1	Record Ho from Step 1, above, and then subtract it from 90° to get the zenith distance	Ho	−		
2-2	Zenith distance	z		°	'

Step 3   Use the Almanac to Find Sun's Declination   GMT date =

					°	'
3-1	Record the date and GMT of the sight (the time the sun reached its peak height)	GMT (hr) =	GMT (min) =			
3-2	Turn to the daily page of the Almanac for the date of the sight, and find the sun's declination (dec) for the hour of the sight (line 3-1) and record it here.	Dec (hr)	N S		°	'
3-3	Record the d-value from the bottom of the dec column in the Almanac. Mark the signs of the d-value and d-corr + if the dec for the next hour is larger, or - if it is smaller.	d-value = + −	d-corr = + −			'
3-4	Turn to the Increments and Corrections pages at the back of the Almanac (T-9 to 12, in the notes) and find the minutes table for the GMT minutes (line 3-1). On the right-hand side of the double line in the table, find the d-corr corresponding to the d-value of line 3-3.	Declination =	N S		°	'
		3-5 Apply the d-corr to the dec(hr) and record it above.				

Step 4   Find Latitude from Zenith Distance and Declination

Record DR Latitude to use as a guide, and then take the sum or difference of zenith distance and declination to find your true Latitude at LAN.

		°	'
Declination or Zenith distance			
Zenith distance or Declination			
Latitude =		°	'

Form 110, for *Polaris* Sights

Step 1. Correct Hs to get Ho					
1-1	Record Sextant Height of *Polaris*	Hs	°		'
1-2	Record Index Correction *"If it's off, put it on; if it's on, take it off."*	Off + On –			'
1-3	Record height of eye (HE=_____) and look up Dip Correction on the right-hand side of Table A2, front of Almanac	Dip –			'
1-4	Sum the above to get the Apparent Height of *Polaris*	Ha	°		'
1-5	Look up the Altitude Correction (always minus)	alt corr.	–		'
1-6	Sum the above two numbers to get Observed Height	Ho	°		'

Step 2. Find LHA Aries (Υ)		UTC Date =		
2-1	UTC Time in Hours, Minutes and Seconds	UTC Time =		
2-2	Find GHA Υ on left-hand side of daily pages of the Nautical Almanac	GHA Υ (hr) =	°	'
2-3	Find GHA Aries minutes and seconds correction from Increments and Corrections pages	GHA Υ (m, s) =	°	'
2-4	Sum the above two numbers to get GHA Aries	GHA Υ =	°	'
	Extra spaces to adjust angles as needed			
2-5	DR Lon: –West; +East	–W, +E	°	'
2-6	Combine 2-4 and 2-5 to get LHA Υ	LHA Υ =	°	'

Step 3. Latitude Determination				
3-1	Ho from 1-6	Ho	°	'
3-2	Subtract 1°		-1 °	
3-3	Add a0 from *Polaris* Table (using LHA Aries)	+a0	°	'
3-4	Add a1 from *Polaris* Table (using DR Latitude)	+a1		'
3-5	Add a2 from *Polaris* Table (using Month)	+a2		'
3-6	Sum the above to find Latitude	Latitude =	°	'
	Note that this procedure for finding Lat from Polaris *is explained in the Nautical Almanac.*			

Form 110, for *Polaris* Sights

Step 1. Correct Hs to get Ho					
1-1	Record Sextant Height of *Polaris*	Hs	°		'
1-2	Record Index Correction *"If it's off, put it on; if it's on, take it off."*	Off + On –			'
1-3	Record height of eye (HE=____) and look up Dip Correction on the right-hand side of Table A2, front of Almanac	Dip –			'
1-4	Sum the above to get the Apparent Height of *Polaris*	Ha	°		'
1-5	Look up the Altitude Correction (always minus)	alt corr.	–		'
1-6	Sum the above two numbers to get Observed Height	Ho	°		'

Step 2. Find LHA Aries (♈)		UTC Date =			
2-1	UTC Time in Hours, Minutes and Seconds	UTC Time =			
2-2	Find GHA ♈ on left-hand side of daily pages of the Nautical Almanac	GHA ♈ (hr) =		°	'
2-3	Find GHA Aries minutes and seconds correction from Increments and Corrections pages	GHA ♈ (m, s) =		°	'
2-4	Sum the above two numbers to get GHA Aries	GHA ♈ =		°	'
	Extra spaces to adjust angles as needed				
2-5	DR Lon: –West; +East	–W, +E		°	'
2-6	Combine 2-4 and 2-5 to get LHA ♈	LHA ♈ =		°	'

Step 3. Latitude Determination					
3-1	Ho from 1-6	Ho	°		'
3-2	Subtract 1°	-1 °			
3-3	Add a0 from *Polaris* Table (using LHA Aries)	+a0	°		'
3-4	Add a1 from *Polaris* Table (using DR Latitude)	+a1			'
3-5	Add a2 from *Polaris* Table (using Month)	+a2			'
3-6	Sum the above to find Latitude	Latitude =	°		'

Note that this procedure for finding Lat from Polaris is explained in the Nautical Almanac.

Form 110, for *Polaris* Sights

Step 1. Correct Hs to get Ho				
1-1	Record Sextant Height of *Polaris*	Hs	°	'
1-2	Record Index Correction *"If it's off, put it on; if it's on, take it off."*	Off + On –		'
1-3	Record height of eye (HE=_____) and look up Dip Correction on the right-hand side of Table A2, front of Almanac	Dip –		'
1-4	Sum the above to get the Apparent Height of *Polaris*	Ha	°	'
1-5	Look up the Altitude Correction (always minus)	alt corr.	–	'
1-6	Sum the above two numbers to get Observed Height	Ho	°	'

Step 2. Find LHA Aries (♈)		UTC Date =		
2-1	UTC Time in Hours, Minutes and Seconds	UTC Time =		
2-2	Find GHA ♈ on left-hand side of daily pages of the Nautical Almanac	GHA ♈ (hr) =	°	'
2-3	Find GHA Aries minutes and seconds correction from Increments and Corrections pages	GHA ♈ (m, s) =	°	'
2-4	Sum the above two numbers to get GHA Aries	GHA ♈ =	°	'
	Extra spaces to adjust angles as needed			
2-5	DR Lon: –West; +East	–W, +E	°	'
2-6	Combine 2-4 and 2-5 to get LHA ♈	LHA ♈ =	°	'

Step 3. Latitude Determination				
3-1	Ho from 1-6	Ho	°	'
3-2	Subtract 1°		-1 °	
3-3	Add a0 from *Polaris* Table (using LHA Aries)	+a0	°	'
3-4	Add a1 from *Polaris* Table (using DR Latitude)	+a1		'
3-5	Add a2 from *Polaris* Table (using Month)	+a2		'
3-6	Sum the above to find Latitude	Latitude =	°	'
Note that this procedure for finding Lat from Polaris *is explained in the Nautical Almanac.*				

Form 110, for *Polaris* Sights

Step 1. Correct Hs to get Ho

			°	'
1-1	Record Sextant Height of *Polaris*	Hs	°	'
1-2	Record Index Correction *"If it's off, put it on; if it's on, take it off."*	Off + On –		'
1-3	Record height of eye (HE=____) and look up Dip Correction on the right-hand side of Table A2, front of Almanac	Dip –		'
1-4	Sum the above to get the Apparent Height of *Polaris*	Ha	°	'
1-5	Look up the Altitude Correction (always minus)	alt corr.	–	'
1-6	Sum the above two numbers to get Observed Height	Ho	°	'

Step 2. Find LHA Aries (♈)

		UTC Date =	°	'
2-1	UTC Time in Hours, Minutes and Seconds	UTC Time =		
2-2	Find GHA ♈ on left-hand side of daily pages of the Nautical Almanac	GHA ♈ (hr) =	°	'
2-3	Find GHA Aries minutes and seconds correction from Increments and Corrections pages	GHA ♈ (m, s) =	°	'
2-4	Sum the above two numbers to get GHA Aries	GHA ♈ =	°	'
	Extra spaces to adjust angles as needed			
2-5	DR Lon: –West; +East	–W, +E	°	'
2-6	Combine 2-4 and 2-5 to get LHA ♈	LHA ♈ =	°	'

Step 3. Latitude Determination

			°	'
3-1	Ho from 1-6	Ho	°	'
3-2	Subtract 1°		-1 °	
3-3	Add a0 from *Polaris* Table (using LHA Aries)	+a0	°	'
3-4	Add a1 from *Polaris* Table (using DR Latitude)	+a1		'
3-5	Add a2 from *Polaris* Table (using Month)	+a2		'
3-6	Sum the above to find Latitude	Latitude =	°	'

Note that this procedure for finding Lat from Polaris is explained in the Nautical Almanac.

Form 110, for *Polaris* Sights

Step 1. Correct Hs to get Ho				
1-1	Record Sextant Height of *Polaris*	Hs	°	'
1-2	Record Index Correction *"If it's off, put it on; if it's on, take it off."*	Off + On –		'
1-3	Record height of eye (HE=_____) and look up Dip Correction on the right-hand side of Table A2, front of Almanac	Dip –		'
1-4	Sum the above to get the Apparent Height of *Polaris*	Ha	°	'
1-5	Look up the Altitude Correction (always minus)	alt corr.	–	'
1-6	Sum the above two numbers to get Observed Height	Ho	°	'

Step 2. Find LHA Aries (♈)		UTC Date =		
2-1	UTC Time in Hours, Minutes and Seconds	UTC Time =		
2-2	Find GHA ♈ on left-hand side of daily pages of the Nautical Almanac	GHA ♈ (hr) =	°	'
2-3	Find GHA Aries minutes and seconds correction from Increments and Corrections pages	GHA ♈ (m, s) =	°	'
2-4	Sum the above two numbers to get GHA Aries	GHA ♈ =	°	'
	Extra spaces to adjust angles as needed			
2-5	DR Lon: –West; +East	–W, +E	°	'
2-6	Combine 2-4 and 2-5 to get LHA ♈	LHA ♈ =	°	'

Step 3. Latitude Determination				
3-1	Ho from 1-6	Ho	°	'
3-2	Subtract 1°		-1 °	
3-3	Add a0 from *Polaris* Table (using LHA Aries)	+a0	°	'
3-4	Add a1 from *Polaris* Table (using DR Latitude)	+a1		'
3-5	Add a2 from *Polaris* Table (using Month)	+a2		'
3-6	Sum the above to find Latitude	Latitude =	°	'

Note that this procedure for finding Lat from Polaris *is explained in the Nautical Almanac.*

Form 110, for *Polaris* Sights

Step 1. Correct Hs to get Ho				
1-1	Record Sextant Height of *Polaris*	Hs	°	'
1-2	Record Index Correction *"If it's off, put it on; if it's on, take it off."*	Off + On –		'
1-3	Record height of eye (HE=____) and look up Dip Correction on the right-hand side of Table A2, front of Almanac	Dip –		'
1-4	Sum the above to get the Apparent Height of *Polaris*	Ha	°	'
1-5	Look up the Altitude Correction (always minus)	alt corr.	–	'
1-6	Sum the above two numbers to get Observed Height	Ho	°	'

Step 2. Find LHA Aries (Υ)		UTC Date =		
2-1	UTC Time in Hours, Minutes and Seconds	UTC Time =		
2-2	Find GHA Υ on left-hand side of daily pages of the Nautical Almanac	GHA Υ (hr) =	°	'
2-3	Find GHA Aries minutes and seconds correction from Increments and Corrections pages	GHA Υ (m, s) =	°	'
2-4	Sum the above two numbers to get GHA Aries	GHA Υ =	°	'
	Extra spaces to adjust angles as needed			
2-5	DR Lon: –West; +East	–W, +E	°	'
2-6	Combine 2-4 and 2-5 to get LHA Υ	LHA Υ =	°	'

Step 3. Latitude Determination				
3-1	Ho from 1-6	Ho	°	'
3-2	Subtract 1°		-1 °	
3-3	Add a0 from *Polaris* Table (using LHA Aries)	+a0	°	'
3-4	Add a1 from *Polaris* Table (using DR Latitude)	+a1		'
3-5	Add a2 from *Polaris* Table (using Month)	+a2		'
3-6	Sum the above to find Latitude	Latitude =	°	'

Note that this procedure for finding Lat from Polaris *is explained in the Nautical Almanac.*

Form 117, Short Forms for LAN and *Polaris* Sights

Lat at LAN			
Find Ho		degrees	minutes
Hs-max =			
IC (+Off, - On) =	±		
Dip (from HE) =	−		
Ha =			
alt corr (UL-,LL+) =	±		
Ho =			
Find z (90°-Ho)		89°	60.0'
Ho =	−		
z =			
DR (Lat, Lon) =			
Lat = sum or difference Dec and z			
Dec or z =			
z or Dec =	±		
Lat =			

Date		hr	min	sec
UTC LAN =				

Declination in Nautical Almanac at UTC of LAN				
		degrees	minutes	d-value (±)
Dec (hr) =	N S			
d corr =	±			
Dec =	N S			

Lon at LAN = GHA sun at UTC of LAN			
		degrees	minutes
GHA (hr) =			
GHA (m.s) =	+		
GHA =			
If GHA between 0 and 180, Lon W = GHA			
If GHA between 180 and 360, Lon E = 360-GHA			

LAN Lat Rules: *For Contrary Name: Lat = z - Dec. For Same Name: DR-Lat > Dec, Lat = z + Dec; DR-Lat < Dec, Lat = Dec -z. But don't forget the easy rule: add them, and if that is nonsense (compared to your DR Lat) then sub-tract them.* **LAN Lon Reminder:** *LAN Lon is only as accurate as the UTC you assign to the event. The Lon will be uncertain by 15' for each 1 minute of time uncertainty in your choice of peak Hs time.*

Find LHA ♈			
UTC *Polaris* sight	hr	min	sec
Date			
DR (Lat, Lon) =			

LHA ♈ = GHA ♈ - Lon W (or + Lon E)			
		degrees	minutes
GHA ♈ (hr) =			
GHA ♈ (m.s) =	+		
GHA ♈ =			
DR Lon (-W,+E) =	±		
LHA ♈ =			
Use LHA ♈ in Polaris Tables to find a0, a1, a2			

Lat by *Polaris*			
		degrees	minutes
Hs of *Polaris* =			
IC (+Off, - On) =	±		
Dip (from HE) =	−		
Ha =			
alt corr =	−		
Ho =			
subtract 1°	−	-1°	
+a0 =	+		
+a1 =	+		
+a2 =	+		
Lat =			

Form 117, Short Forms for LAN and *Polaris* Sights

Lat at LAN			
Find Ho		degrees	minutes
Hs-max =			
IC (+Off, - On) =	±		
Dip (from HE) =	−		
Ha =			
alt corr (UL-,LL+) =	±		
Ho =			
Find z (90°-Ho)		89°	60.0'
Ho =	−		
z =			
DR (Lat, Lon) =			
Lat = sum or difference Dec and z			
Dec or z =			
z or Dec =	±		
Lat =			

Date		hr	min	sec
UTC LAN =				

Declination in Nautical Almanac at UTC of LAN				
		degrees	minutes	d-value (±)
Dec (hr) =	N S			
d corr =	±			
Dec =	N S			

Lon at LAN = GHA sun at UTC of LAN			
		degrees	minutes
GHA (hr) =			
GHA (m.s) =	+		
GHA =			
If GHA between 0 and 180, Lon W = GHA			
If GHA between 180 and 360, Lon E = 360-GHA			

LAN Lat Rules: *For Contrary Name: Lat = z - Dec. For Same Name: DR-Lat > Dec, Lat = z + Dec; DR-Lat < Dec, Lat = Dec -z. But don't forget the easy rule: add them, and if that is nonsense (compared to your DR Lat) then sub-tract them.* **LAN Lon Reminder:** *LAN Lon is only as accurate as the UTC you assign to the event. The Lon will be uncertain by 15' for each 1 minute of time uncertainty in your choice of peak Hs time.*

Find LHA ♈			
UTC *Polaris* sight	hr	min	sec
Date			
DR (Lat, Lon) =			

LHA ♈ = GHA ♈ - Lon W (or + Lon E)			
		degrees	minutes
GHA ♈ (hr) =			
GHA ♈ (m.s) =	+		
GHA ♈ =			
DR Lon (-W,+E) =	±		
LHA ♈ =			
Use LHA ♈ in Polaris Tables to find a0, a1, a2			

Lat by *Polaris*			
		degrees	minutes
Hs of *Polaris* =			
IC (+Off, - On) =	±		
Dip (from HE) =	−		
Ha =			
alt corr =	−		
Ho =			
subtract 1°	−	-1°	
+a0 =	+		
+a1 =	+		
+a2 =	+		
Lat =			

Form 117, Short Forms for LAN and *Polaris* Sights

Lat at LAN			
Find Ho		degrees	minutes
Hs-max =			
IC (+Off, - On) =	±		
Dip (from HE) =	−		
Ha =			
alt corr (UL-,LL+) =	±		
Ho =			
Find z (90°-Ho)		89°	60.0'
Ho =	−		
z =			
DR (Lat, Lon) =			
Lat = sum or difference Dec and z			
Dec or z =			
z or Dec =	±		
Lat =			

Date		hr	min	sec
UTC LAN =				

Declination in Nautical Almanac at UTC of LAN				
		degrees	minutes	d-value (±)
Dec (hr) =	N S			
d corr =	±			
Dec =	N S			

Lon at LAN = GHA sun at UTC of LAN			
		degrees	minutes
GHA (hr) =			
GHA (m.s) =	+		
GHA =			
If GHA between 0 and 180, Lon W = GHA			
If GHA between 180 and 360, Lon E = 360-GHA			

LAN Lat Rules: *For Contrary Name: Lat = z - Dec. For Same Name: DR-Lat > Dec, Lat = z + Dec; DR-Lat < Dec, Lat = Dec -z. But don't forget the easy rule: add them, and if that is nonsense (compared to your DR Lat) then sub-tract them.* **LAN Lon Reminder:** *LAN Lon is only as accurate as the UTC you assign to the event. The Lon will be uncertain by 15' for each 1 minute of time uncertainty in your choice of peak Hs time.*

Find LHA ♈			
UTC *Polaris* sight	hr	min	sec
Date			
DR (Lat, Lon) =			

LHA ♈ = GHA ♈ - Lon W (or + Lon E)			
		degrees	minutes
GHA ♈ (hr) =			
GHA ♈ (m.s) =	+		
GHA ♈ =			
DR Lon (-W,+E) =	±		
LHA ♈ =			
Use LHA ♈ in Polaris Tables to find a0, a1, a2			

Lat by *Polaris*			
		degrees	minutes
Hs of *Polaris* =			
IC (+Off, - On) =	±		
Dip (from HE) =	−		
Ha =			
alt corr =	−		
Ho =			
subtract 1°	−	-1°	
+a0 =	+		
+a1 =	+		
+a2 =	+		
Lat =			

Form 117, Short Forms for LAN and *Polaris* Sights

Lat at LAN			
Find Ho		degrees	minutes
Hs-max =			
IC (+Off, - On) =	±		
Dip (from HE) =	−		
Ha =			
alt corr (UL-,LL+) =	±		
Ho =			
Find z (90°-Ho)		89°	60.0'
Ho =	−		
z =			
DR (Lat, Lon) =			
Lat = sum or difference Dec and z			
Dec or z =			
z or Dec =	±		
Lat =			

Date		hr	min	sec
UTC LAN =				

Declination in Nautical Almanac at UTC of LAN					
		degrees	minutes	d-value (±)	
Dec (hr) =	N S				
d corr =	±				
Dec =	N S				

Lon at LAN = GHA sun at UTC of LAN			
		degrees	minutes
GHA (hr) =			
GHA (m.s) =	+		
GHA =			
If GHA between 0 and 180, Lon W = GHA			
If GHA between 180 and 360, Lon E = 360-GHA			

LAN Lat Rules: *For Contrary Name: Lat = z - Dec. For Same Name: DR-Lat > Dec, Lat = z + Dec; DR-Lat < Dec, Lat = Dec -z. But don't forget the easy rule: add them, and if that is nonsense (compared to your DR Lat) then sub-tract them.* **LAN Lon Reminder:** *LAN Lon is only as accurate as the UTC you assign to the event. The Lon will be uncertain by 15' for each 1 minute of time uncertainty in your choice of peak Hs time.*

Find LHA ♈				
UTC *Polaris* sight		hr	min	sec
Date				
DR (Lat, Lon) =				

LHA ♈ = GHA ♈ - Lon W (or + Lon E)			
		degrees	minutes
GHA ♈ (hr) =			
GHA ♈ (m.s) =	+		
GHA ♈ =			
DR Lon (-W,+E) =	±		
LHA ♈ =			
Use LHA ♈ in Polaris Tables to find a0, a1, a2			

Lat by *Polaris*			
		degrees	minutes
Hs of *Polaris* =			
IC (+Off, - On) =	±		
Dip (from HE) =	−		
Ha =			
alt corr =	−		
Ho =			
subtract 1°	−	-1°	
+a0 =	+		
+a1 =	+		
+a2 =	+		
Lat =			

Form 117, Short Forms for LAN and *Polaris* Sights

Lat at LAN			
Find Ho		degrees	minutes
Hs-max =			
IC (+Off, - On) =	±		
Dip (from HE) =	−		
Ha =			
alt corr (UL-,LL+) =	±		
Ho =			
Find z (90°-Ho)		89°	60.0'
Ho =	−		
z =			
DR (Lat, Lon) =			
Lat = sum or difference Dec and z			
Dec or z =			
z or Dec =	±		
Lat =			

Date		hr	min	sec
UTC LAN =				

Declaration in Nautical Almanac at UTC of LAN					
		degrees	minutes	d-value (±)	
Dec (hr) =	N S				
d corr =	±				
Dec =	N S				

Lon at LAN = GHA sun at UTC of LAN			
		degrees	minutes
GHA (hr) =			
GHA (m.s) =	+		
GHA =			
If GHA between 0 and 180, Lon W = GHA			
If GHA between 180 and 360, Lon E = 360-GHA			

LAN Lat Rules: *For Contrary Name: Lat = z - Dec. For Same Name: DR-Lat > Dec, Lat = z + Dec; DR-Lat < Dec, Lat = Dec -z. But don't forget the easy rule: add them, and if that is nonsense (compared to your DR Lat) then sub-tract them.* **LAN Lon Reminder:** *LAN Lon is only as accurate as the UTC you assign to the event. The Lon will be uncertain by 15' for each 1 minute of time uncertainty in your choice of peak Hs time.*

Find LHA ♈			
UTC *Polaris* sight	hr	min	sec
Date			
DR (Lat, Lon) =			

LHA ♈ = GHA ♈ - Lon W (or + Lon E)			
		degrees	minutes
GHA ♈ (hr) =			
GHA ♈ (m.s) =	+		
GHA ♈ =			
DR Lon (-W,+E) =	±		
LHA ♈ =			
Use LHA ♈ in Polaris Tables to find a0, a1, a2			

Lat by *Polaris*			
		degrees	minutes
Hs of *Polaris* =			
IC (+Off, - On) =	±		
Dip (from HE) =	−		
Ha =			
alt corr =	−		
Ho =			
subtract 1°	−	-1°	
+a0 =	+		
+a1 =	+		
+a2 =	+		
Lat =			

Form 117, Short Forms for LAN and *Polaris* Sights

Lat at LAN		degrees	minutes
Find Ho		degrees	minutes
Hs-max =			
IC (+Off, - On) =	±		
Dip (from HE) =	−		
Ha =			
alt corr (UL-,LL+) =	±		
Ho =			
Find z (90°-Ho)		89°	60.0'
Ho =	−		
z =			
DR (Lat, Lon) =			
Lat = sum or difference Dec and z			
Dec or z =			
z or Dec =	±		
Lat =			

Date		hr	min	sec
UTC LAN =				

Declination in Nautical Almanac at UTC of LAN			degrees	minutes	d-value (±)
Dec (hr) =	N S				
d corr =	±				
Dec =	N S				

Lon at LAN = GHA sun at UTC of LAN		degrees	minutes
GHA (hr) =			
GHA (m.s) =	+		
GHA =			
If GHA between 0 and 180, Lon W = GHA			
If GHA between 180 and 360, Lon E = 360-GHA			

LAN Lat Rules: *For Contrary Name: Lat = z - Dec. For Same Name: DR-Lat > Dec, Lat = z + Dec; DR-Lat < Dec, Lat = Dec -z. But don't forget the easy rule: add them, and if that is nonsense (compared to your DR Lat) then sub-tract them.* **LAN Lon Reminder:** *LAN Lon is only as accurate as the UTC you assign to the event. The Lon will be uncertain by 15' for each 1 minute of time uncertainty in your choice of peak Hs time.*

Find LHA ♈	hr	min	sec
UTC *Polaris* sight			
Date			
DR (Lat, Lon) =			

LHA ♈ = GHA ♈ - Lon W (or + Lon E)		degrees	minutes
GHA ♈ (hr) =			
GHA ♈ (m.s) =	+		
GHA ♈ =			
DR Lon (-W,+E) =	±		
LHA ♈ =			
Use LHA ♈ in Polaris Tables to find a0, a1, a2			

Lat by *Polaris*		degrees	minutes
Hs of *Polaris* =			
IC (+Off, - On) =	±		
Dip (from HE) =	−		
Ha =			
alt corr =	−		
Ho =			
subtract 1°	−	-1°	
+a0 =	+		
+a1 =	+		
+a2 =	+		
Lat =			

Form 111, for Pub. 249, Volume 1, Selected Stars

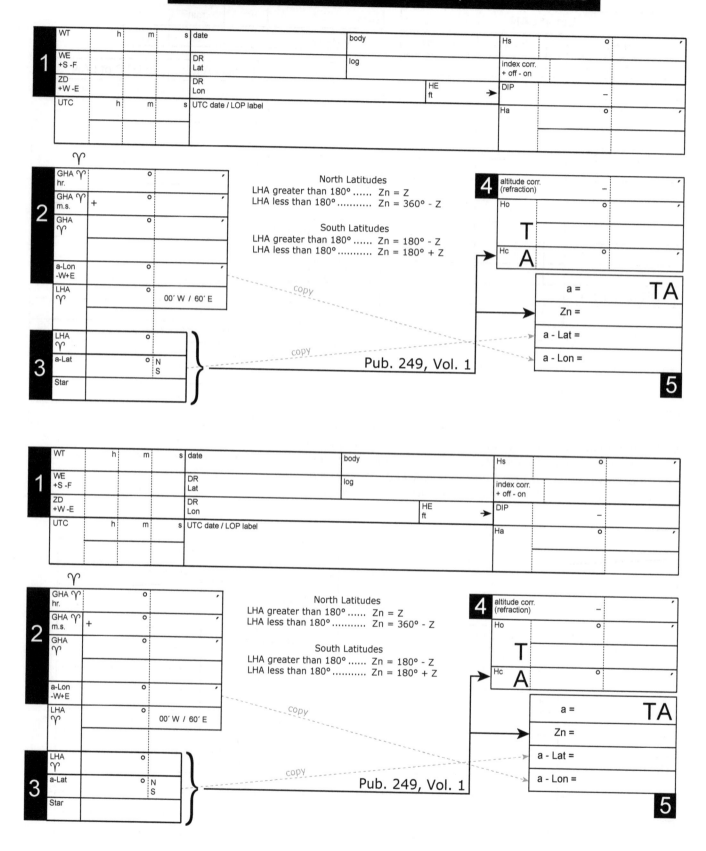

North Latitudes
LHA greater than 180° ...... Zn = Z
LHA less than 180° .... Zn = 360° - Z

South Latitudes
LHA greater than 180° ...... Zn = 180° - Z
LHA less than 180° .... Zn = 180° + Z

Pub. 249, Vol. 1

Form 111, for Pub. 249, Volume 1, Selected Stars

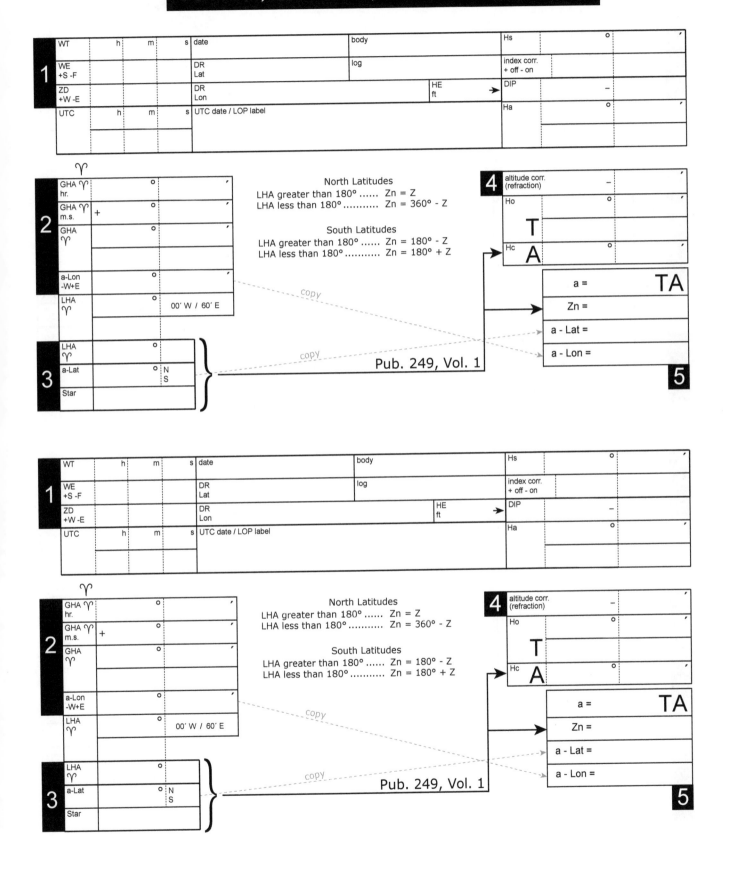

North Latitudes
LHA greater than 180° ...... Zn = Z
LHA less than 180° .... Zn = 360° - Z

South Latitudes
LHA greater than 180° ...... Zn = 180° - Z
LHA less than 180° .... Zn = 180° + Z

Pub. 249, Vol. 1

Form 111, for Pub. 249, Volume 1, Selected Stars

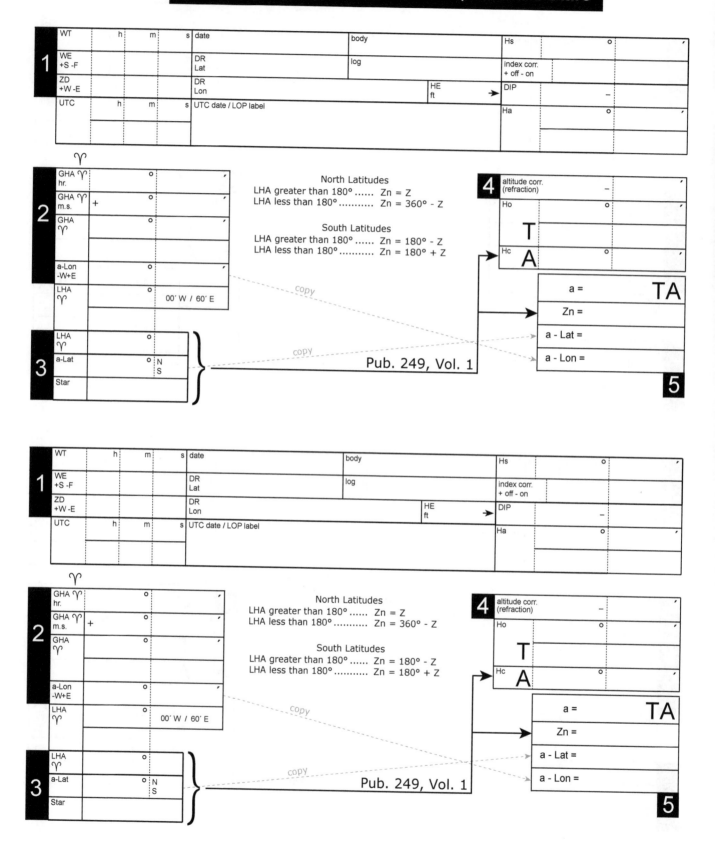

1
WT		h	m	s	date		body		Hs		°		'
WE +S -F					DR Lat		log		index corr. + off - on				
ZD +W -E					DR Lon		HE ft	→	DIP			−	
UTC		h	m	s	UTC date / LOP label				Ha		°		'

2
GHA ♈ hr.		°		'
GHA ♈ m.s.	+	°		'
GHA ♈		°		'
a-Lon -W+E		°		'
LHA ♈		°	00′ W / 60′ E	

North Latitudes
LHA greater than 180° ...... Zn = Z
LHA less than 180° .... Zn = 360° - Z

South Latitudes
LHA greater than 180° ...... Zn = 180° - Z
LHA less than 180° .... Zn = 180° + Z

3
LHA ♈		°
a-Lat		° N / S
Star		

copy   *copy*   Pub. 249, Vol. 1

4
altitude corr. (refraction)		−	
Ho		°	'
Hc		°	'

T A

5
a =	TA
Zn =	
a - Lat =	
a - Lon =	

1
WT		h	m	s	date		body		Hs		°		'
WE +S -F					DR Lat		log		index corr. + off - on				
ZD +W -E					DR Lon		HE ft	→	DIP			−	
UTC		h	m	s	UTC date / LOP label				Ha		°		'

2
GHA ♈ hr.		°		'
GHA ♈ m.s.	+	°		'
GHA ♈		°		'
a-Lon -W+E		°		'
LHA ♈		°	00′ W / 60′ E	

North Latitudes
LHA greater than 180° ...... Zn = Z
LHA less than 180° .... Zn = 360° - Z

South Latitudes
LHA greater than 180° ...... Zn = 180° - Z
LHA less than 180° .... Zn = 180° + Z

3
LHA ♈		°
a-Lat		° N / S
Star		

copy   *copy*   Pub. 249, Vol. 1

4
altitude corr. (refraction)		−	
Ho		°	'
Hc		°	'

T A

5
a =	TA
Zn =	
a - Lat =	
a - Lon =	

Form 111, for Pub. 249, Volume 1, Selected Stars

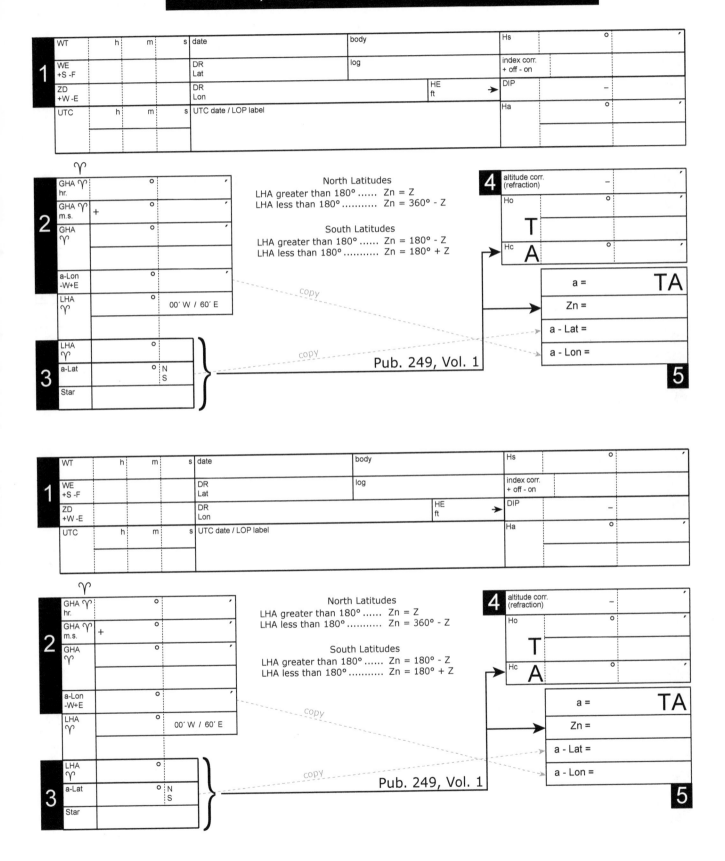

84

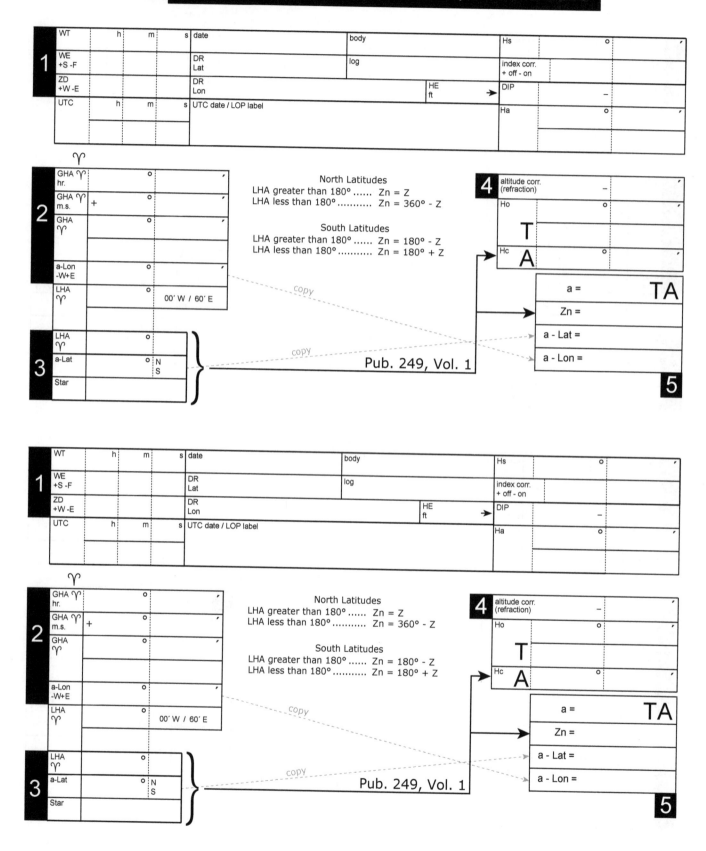

Form 111, for Pub. 249, Volume 1, Selected Stars

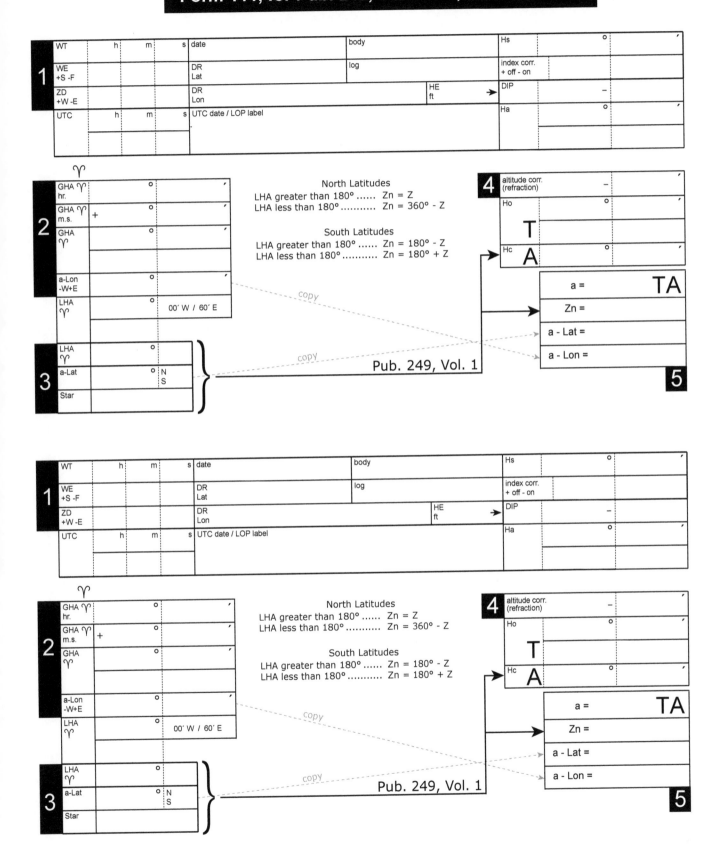

North Latitudes
LHA greater than 180° ...... Zn = Z
LHA less than 180° .... Zn = 360° - Z

South Latitudes
LHA greater than 180° ...... Zn = 180° - Z
LHA less than 180° .... Zn = 180° + Z

Pub. 249, Vol. 1

North Latitudes
LHA greater than 180° ...... Zn = Z
LHA less than 180° .... Zn = 360° - Z

South Latitudes
LHA greater than 180° ...... Zn = 180° - Z
LHA less than 180° .... Zn = 180° + Z

Pub. 249, Vol. 1